ANYTHING'S POSSIBLE:
THE 47-DAY PROPHECY

Evelyn Murray Drayton

ANYTHING'S POSSIBLE: THE 47-DAY PROPHECY

Evelyn Murray Drayton

Sellrus Publishing

Georgetown, South Carolina

ANYTHING'S POSSIBLE: THE 47-DAY PROPHECY
Copyright © 2015 Evelyn Murray Drayton.

All rights reserved. No part of this book may be used or reproduced by any means, graphic, electronic, or mechanical, including photocopying, recording, taping, or by any information storage retrieval system without the written permission of the publisher or the author, except in the case of brief quotations embodied in critical articles and reviews. Neither Sellrus Publishing nor the author is responsible for errors or omissions, nor liable for damages resulting from use of information contained therein.

Unless otherwise indicated, all scripture quotations are taken from the King James Version of The New Open Bible (1990). Nashville, TN: Thomas Nelson, Inc.

Books may be ordered through booksellers or by contacting:
 Sellrus Publishing
 876 Ford Village Road
 Georgetown, SC 29440
 843-546-4057

Book Cover Design: "Timeless Rose"
Courtesy of Holly Cawfield Photography

Web addresses or links mentioned in this book may have changed since publication due to the dynamic nature of the Internet.

ISBN: 978-1-943385-00-3 (sc)
ISBN: 978-1-943385-01-0 (e)

Library of Congress Control Number: 2015917837

Printed in the United States of America

Sellrus Publishing rev. date: 11/15/2015

Contents

Acknowledgments vii

Introduction ix

Chapter 1 From Tragedy to Triumph 1

Chapter 2 God Restores Health 61

Chapter 3 Pleasant Dreams 105

Chapter 4 Power of Healing Words and Deeds ..131

Chapter 5 Endless Possibilities 151

Chapter 6 A Recipe For Healing 161

Conclusion 169

Personal Examination 175

About the Author 181

Acknowledgments

I honor my husband, Russell, for his support and loyalty as I recovered from the near-fatal vehicle accident that occurred in June 2013. When he was diagnosed with cancer several years ago, God spared his life. I truly thank God for him being here to help me during my time of need. My two boys, Justin and Nicholas, were there for me as well. As a team, they proved to me over and over that love is more than mere words; love, indeed, is action.

I thank God for many church groups that included me on their prayer lists. It was an honor to have shared my testimony with several of those congregations. I bless the Lord for each person who has touched my life and was instrumental in praying for my recuperation from the near-death experience. I gladly and humbly honor all to whom honor is due. Though I am appreciative of the many prayers and kind deeds, I am constantly reminded that only God gets the glory and honor for the great work He is doing in my life.

I am honored that God has given me life and allowed me the opportunity to write another book, my eighth. I am grateful for Mr. Clayton Stairs of Pawleys Island, South Carolina, who has been instrumental in providing editing services for this project.

God is keeping me in perfect peace. Surely, goodness and mercy are following me and I am still dwelling in the house of the Lord.

"This is the Lord's doing; it is marvelous in our eyes" (Psalm 118:23).

Introduction

"Many are the afflictions of the righteous: but the Lord delivereth him out of them all" (Psalm 34:19).

It is an honor to share my story of tragedy to triumph in ***Anything's Possible: The 47-Day Prophecy.*** I recount a June 2013 near-fatal accident caused by a head-on collision. A few hours prior to the auto collision, I was given a prophetic word that tremendously impacted my life. I had a ***Day 47*** experience incited by a prophetic word and knowledge of God's plan for me! Having survived the near-death experience has brought about a change in my life. I know for sure now that the spiritual gift of prophecy is real.

I have learned that love for others is not dependent on their love for me. Love is not based on what people can do for me, but on the love within my heart for them. Not everyone has to experience a traumatic event in order to know how to love others, but one of my greatest changes is loving people in a greater way. I love God's creation—I love people in deed and truth! I speak of love so much these days, it may seem disingenuous to some. Frankly, loving others is the right thing to do!

The most empowering moment for me is when I talk about our Father's love. In spite of bad things that happen to us, He still loves us. Interestingly, I talk about infinite possibilities when we depend on God to help us accomplish His purpose of love and life through us. Let us not wait for disaster to draw us together to express love.

Our Godly testimonies are structured to help encourage others to keep a survival frame of mind. Survival is the love given to us from our Heavenly Father. An exhilarating and liberating mindset ushers us to a place of sharing and praising God for the ways He allows us to pen some of His mighty acts in life.

I take on the awesome task of discussing love, healing, prophecy, and forgiveness. My triumphant story will encourage and strengthen each person as you read words from my heart—and some straight from the heart of our Heavenly Father.

Come and walk with me on this epic adventure as I share some of my amazing triumphs in life. If you noticed, I did not say walk *for* me; I only want you to walk alongside me. Let's go!

Chapter One

From Tragedy to Triumph

"If thou canst believe, all things are possible to him that believeth"
(Mark 9:23).

People all over the world experience trauma every day. We are all created equal and there is no line of demarcation for troubling experiences in life. Some people are strong enough to face their challenges and keep on living. Sadly, many people become weary and relent to a nefarious life during their struggle, only to suffer defeat. Ironically, though, when we share our testimony of survival, other people can benefit by realizing they are not alone in their situations.

Speaking of trauma, one of my most challenging experiences took place on June 2, 2013, when I was involved in a horrific head-on collision. We tend to tell each other to buckle up and be careful when driving on the dangerous highways—and I believe I was driving safely. I was not talking on the cell phone nor was I texting. The police report indicates I was not speeding or drinking and driving. I was not sleeping either! Yet I was involved in this near-fatal vehicle accident. I will not discuss the impairment of the other driver; but I guess I did not watch out for the other guy!

Evelyn Murray Drayton

Prior to the accident and throughout the upcoming months, I was scheduled for various speaking and singing engagements. While I was scheduling and planning, so was Satan. He does not fight fairly. Satan tries to catch us with our guard down and uses tricks to instigate temptation, rebellion, and hardships. He caught me off guard this day because a vehicle accident was the last thing on my mind as I updated my calendar of events. I am just a babe in the music arena, but my promotional engagements had already proliferated when my name was circulated alongside well-known singers on various flyers. I was even scheduled to participate on stage with some legendary singers. I was not egotistical, but rather excited about my involvement in blessing the Body of Christ. In addition to the singing engagements, I was also booked for several speaking engagements. As a matter of fact, I was scheduled for speaking engagements on Monday, June 3, and on Wednesday, June 5; but I was involved in the near-fatal accident on Sunday evening, June 2. Most of my supporters had not yet heard the terrible news about my horrific accident that clashed with my scheduled events. As a matter of fact, several people told me they learned of my tragedy when they showed up for my June 3 event.

Most hardships and challenges enter our lives unannounced. I woke up early Sunday morning, June 2, 2013, with sound mind and in good health. While staring through the window enjoying the bright sunshine, I was excited to start the day. I suddenly had this whim to fulfill a promise I had made to visit a friend's church and thought today would be the perfect day to do so. Instead of attending church locally, as usual, I prepared to fellowship with my friend and his family located at 1335 Golf Terrace Road in Florence, South Carolina, about 65 miles away from my house. I spent a few minutes printing the directions as a backup to my installed GPS and was set for the highway. Instead of hot curling my freshly washed and dyed hair, I chose to wear one of my fancy wigs. My nails had been professionally manicured two days earlier, so getting ready was a piece of cake. I took my time getting dressed, knowing that I had enough time for the drive since it was an afternoon church service. For some unknown reason, though, I changed handbags and organized the contents. I made sure I had separated my driver's license, vehicle registration, and insurance cards for easy retrieval. *Why did I separate my identification cards?*

I was not apprehensive about starting my day, nor do I recall a premonition indicative of my solitude in a medical facility, but *there must have been a reason that I separated my identification cards.* I did not know that I was preparing those cards for emergency medical workers and highway patrolmen. Oh, there was one other thing I did that was unusual—I changed the complete bedding in the room that my nephew John-Michael once occupied when he lived with us. *Why did I change the bedding in this room this day?* I did not know that I prepared this bed to occupy after my hospital release. My bedroom has an antiquated semiwaveless waterbed I could not sleep in with a broken backbone and other broken parts. Little did I know that I would not independently walk through the doors of my house anytime soon! Unwittingly, the events of this day subsequently led to a near-death experience, hospitalization, debilitating pain, and an agonizing recovery! **The accident didn't surprise God—can you see what I see thus far?**

Having a propensity for safe driving and timely arrival, I proudly arrived in Florence ahead of time for my friend's afternoon religious service. To my surprise, several other vehicles were already in the parking lot, but I decided to sit in my vehicle to observe any newcomers. Warmth from the bright sunshine forced me to exit the vehicle and enter the facility sooner than anticipated. Once inside the building, I realized that another ministry shared the same edifice and the pastor was already standing to conclude the worship experience. Since this was my first time visiting this place, I sat inconspicuously in the back row while the pastor offered a benediction to end the services.

Evelyn Murray Drayton

After the benediction, the pastor immediately approached me and told me that God had spoken to him about me. I had never seen this man before and was not impressed that one more person could tell me he had heard from God. I did not want to appear gullible and hungry for a prophetic word. I later found out that this leader was none other than native South Carolinian **Apostle Lance R. Jeter**, pastor of Restoration Tabernacle and presiding prelate of Shekinah Fellowship of Churches. He has served as a school district superintendent, is a prolific Bible college professor, and has a wealth of experience in church leadership. I did not realize at the time that I was in the midst of such greatness, but I believe it was ordained by God that our paths crossed.

As I listened, Apostle Jeter told me several things that were important to my faith walk. The words spoken to me were not gratuitously given because I know God speaks with purpose. He told me that the enemy tried to steal from me, but there would be a turnaround in my ministry after **47** days. Amidst all his other prophetic words, the pastor was precise and adamant about the number 47. I grabbed a napkin from my pocketbook to record the words of Apostle Jeter, but in haste wrote 45 days instead of 47 as he had stated. Although my notes were not all-encompassing, I corrected the number to 47, recorded a few more credulous words, and stuck the napkin back into my pocketbook. I had hoped that I did not misconstrue the prophecy. I immediately retrieved and perused my notes, and thought to myself, *"What can possibly happen in 47 days that would significantly impact the assignment on my life?"* (Stay with me for a while…I share the significance of the number **47**. Keep reading!)

Apostle Jeter's assistant pastor came over to greet me. As we greeted, she recognized my name and recalled the two of us had discussed a singing engagement over the telephone several months earlier. We were both honored to finally put a face to each other's voice. Subsequent to our meeting, she invited me to dine about an hour or so later with her church family, an invitation I gladly accepted. My friend's service and the dinner would follow immediately at this same facility.

Shortly following the dinner acceptance, my friend showed up with his congregation. I had already received the prophecy and the dinner invitation, so I wondered what would ensue next. My friend and a few other people greeted me as I was ushered to the pulpit for the unity services of prayer, preaching, and singing. I remember standing at the podium, but I don't recall whether I decided to pray or to make remarks. At the end of the service, all the clergy descended the podium and marched out of the sanctuary. Now it was time to eat!

The décor and food aroma created a royal ambience as I was escorted and served in a queenly fashion. That whiff had me salivating before I reached the table. While I probably did not have a voracious appetite, I enjoyed the onsite preparation of piping hot baked ham, turkey with dressing, macaroni and cheese, etc. This dinner was the best-tasting meal I had ever eaten. Naïve to such esteem, I thought, "*God, what have I done to receive this great and sudden honor?*" Surprisingly, I don't recall what happened during or after the meal.

In retrospect, I don't recall leaving the church facility. However, upon my departure and driving over 30 miles toward home, I was involved in a near-fatal vehicle accident. It was later shared with my husband that someone falsely told the highway patrolman that he or she *saw* me hit the other vehicle. I thank God for investigators who know how to determine the exact cause of accidents. I am grateful that a copy of the official police report is in my possession.

The rather bizarre accident took place within only a few hours of the prophecy spoken to me. My sports utility vehicle (SUV) was hit head-on by a pickup truck, breaking my back, pelvis, and a leg. I also had other injuries. I spent nearly three weeks in a medically induced coma as my family wondered whether I would survive or would ever be the same. It was a miracle I survived; but, at the time, my calamity seemed like a nightmare to them!

Unfortunately, the other driver, who caused the accident, died at the scene, but I didn't know. I did not find out until July 4, 2013, right at a month later, that the driver of the other vehicle died instantly at the scene of the accident amid the pouring rain. My husband attended the deceased man's funeral. I later mourned the catastrophic outcome of the fatally wounded young man. As I recovered from my injuries, I telephoned the deceased driver's wife to offer my belated condolences.

About eighteen months after the accident I visited the church where the deceased driver was eulogized and identified myself to the pastor and congregants. With humility, I shared some details of my survival and showed them my miraculous healing. Immediately after that church service, one of the members (who is also a relative of the deceased driver) informed me that she arrived at the accident scene just before the Rescue Squad departed with me, en route to the hospital. She had seen the damage to my vehicle and was blessed to see me alive and doing well.

> *"And it shall come to pass, that before they call, I will answer; and while they are yet speaking, I will hear"* (Isaiah 65:24).

McLeod Regional Medical Center

The accident happened near Johnsonville in Florence County, South Carolina. Based on the police report, there was a direct hit to my vehicle on the driver's side. Records indicate that I was pinned in my vehicle for about 30 minutes while equipment called Jaws of Life was used to extricate me.

Anything's Possible: The 47-Day Prophecy

God spared my life June 2, 2013

    My son, Justin, was able to snap a picture of my demolished vehicle. The other driver's damaged vehicle depicted a white towel covering the driver-side window. It is my understanding that the draped towel indicated he had died. Justin's photo revealed a white towel on my vehicle, but it was still folded on the roof of my SUV, instead of covering my vehicle—Thank God. I often wondered how and why I survived, but I know God knows all about it.

    I don't know any details about the impact of the two vehicles. It seems I was knocked senseless. What I know is what I was told and what I have read from many pages of medical records and police reports. After prolonged extrication from my SUV, paramedics transported me to the emergency room at McLeod Regional Medical Center in Florence. I left the scene unconscious, but apparently regained consciousness prior to my arrival at the hospital. My major complaint in the ambulance was abdominal pain, which was due to blunt force trauma to my stomach. Emergency department medical records indicate that upon arrival, miraculously, I was alert and answering questions intelligently. Interestingly, my medical records indicate that I identified the medicine I am allergic to and told the staff that I am an occasional smoking diabetic! I must have been distraught because I am not a smoker nor do I have diabetes. So, yes, something was undeniably wrong with my brain. But at least I was able to talk! *I definitely need to request expurgation of my medical records though!*

My memory was impaired due to a traumatic brain injury; but, **Shirley Davis of Johnsonville, South Carolina,** the first known person to arrive at the scene, later shared some treasured information with me. Shirley found me alert in the crashed vehicle and made verbal contact with me. She said I told her, *"I'm ready to get out of this vehicle."* She stated how she retrieved my cell phone and requested my emergency contact number. I consciously—in spite of my massive injuries—provided the cell phone number for my husband, Russell, to inform him of the accident. I frequently transposed his cellular telephone number, so I was amazed when Shirley said she reached my husband on the first attempt. I know my comprehension was God's divine intervention! I am so grateful how God used this woman to come to my rescue. *Why don't I remember any of this?*

When Shirley contacted Russell, he was practicing guitar lessons at the home of a church member. He immediately left practice while diligently trying to contact our two sons. Calls to our younger son, Nicholas, were dropped, so he didn't know about the accident until later that night. Russell was able, however, to contact our older son, Justin, who accompanied him to the accident scene. I have realized that the same way calls to Nicholas were dropped, this dilemma could have transpired when Shirley tried to contact my husband about the accident. My life is in God's hands and I thank Him for the divine connection.

Shirley could not tell my husband the severity of the accident; she didn't know either. Russell said he assumed it was only a fender bender since I was alert and talking. By the time Russell and Justin had driven to the scene, I had been extricated from my vehicle and taken to the emergency room. Nurses told Russell and Justin upon their arrival at the hospital that they could not see me because the doctors were trying to stabilize me. Russell said they sat in the waiting area for over five hours while the doctors were feverishly examining my battered frame. Then a team of doctors finally came out and rendered a grim prognosis. They told my husband and son that it didn't look good. They had only begun to elucidate what steps they would take to preserve my life. **Preserve my life?** *What happened to me from the time I gave Shirley the telephone number until my arrival at the emergency room? What happened from the time I was in the emergency room, talking deliriously, until the time I was placed on life support?* **Life support?**

While it was obvious my left femur was broken and both legs suffered damage, emergency room workers could not immediately detect the other life-threatening broken and battered internal injuries. Records indicate that my words became slurred as my condition worsened. As my condition deteriorated while in the emergency room, I was rushed to the trauma unit. During the night I suffered acute respiratory failure with panic episodes, agitation, and mental status changes. After the doctors' assessment, they again released a gloomy prognosis to my husband that they could not guarantee saving my life. They thought I would flatline at any moment! I was indeed dying and they had to perform aggressive resuscitation.

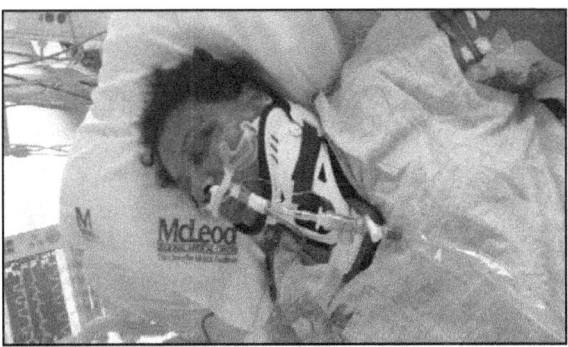

Death was knocking on my door, June 2013

I don't recall seeing any bright lights in a tunnel or any other scenes normally reported with near-death experiences. If I experienced those revelatory moments, I do not recall them; I figuratively and literally stared into death's door as I watched the angels fight for my life.

My major injuries included: bleeding on the brain, broken back, broken pelvis, broken left femur, badly bruised lungs, lacerated liver, numerous fractured ribs, and pneumonia. The doctors feared brain damage and perhaps a spinal cord injury. According to physicians, one wrong move and I could have been paralyzed for life, or with one wrong move I could have been dead. From the onset, it appeared I was only a half-breath away from dying. For a considerable time there had been no viable alternative to keep me alive. Doctors were unsure if I would survive, but were persistent in stabilizing me. I was put under a medically induced coma and remained on life support for nearly three weeks. Multiple required surgeries could not be performed in rapid succession. Consequently, doctors began the arduous task of repairing internal and external injuries by spreading out the surgeries over several days. A feeding tube or stomach peg (percutaneous endoscopic gastrostomy) was inserted while I lay in a comatose condition and was required during the duration of my hospital stay. The feeding tube remained in my stomach until the day I was transferred from the hospital to rehab. I thank God for how He uses accessible medical technology to help preserve lives. God is awesome!

This unprecedented dilemma for my family was dramatic, as well as traumatic. Both Justin and Nicholas were perplexed! Justin had just started his new summer job and Nicholas was scheduled to matriculate at truck drivers' training the same week. My almost-grief-stricken husband, though distraught, was the glue for all the forthcoming episodes. They were not prepared for the tumultuous sequence of events that happened so suddenly. I entered the emergency room talking. Now, with a respirator down my throat and multiple surgeries later, doctors didn't know if I would live or die; whether I would be permanently brain damaged if I lived—they did not know. The family structure changed in one day and was filled with questions—but they still had hope for a better day. *How can this be?*

Scripture tells us, *"Call unto me"* (Jeremiah 33:3). We must always call on our Heavenly Father with the belief that prayer changes things. While simultaneously praying and hearing the bad news coming from the medical staff, it seemed only natural to face the facts and inform other family members of the situation. Desperate phone calls were made to family members stating the severity of the accident and the dire need of prayer for my life.

In addition to updating family members, Russell also notified a few other local people. Several of them extended love and kindness through visits, despite visitation restrictions. My friend, **Mary Geddis Canteen,** was also informed about my mishap. She is a former coworker whom I love and consider as dear to me as a sister—and Russell knew this. Mary is a beautiful young woman with a pleasant personality and an effervescent smile. Initially, hospital visitation was limited to immediate family only, but Mary and her husband, **James Canteen,** rushed to my bedside and offered me their incalculable support every step of the way. I appreciate how James worked cooperatively with Mary to schedule the extra travel time to visit me after their long day of work. She even kept many of my former coworkers updated on my condition. I had no idea that she had chronicled my medical progression until after my hospital release. Thankfully, Mary's hospital visits and administrative skills proved beneficial to me for my manuscript. These are several notes that Mary compiled:

Sent: Monday, June 03, 2013
Evelyn was in a serious accident yesterday afternoon and is listed in critical condition at the McLeod Hospital in Florence. The next two days are very crucial for her. I spoke with her husband Russell this morning and he said she has a lot of broken bones, bleeding on the brain, her liver is damaged, her spine is damaged, her hip is broken,

etc. The accident happened near Johnsonville going towards Kingsburg. It was raining very hard and a truck hydroplaned and hit her. The impact of the accident crushed her car so badly that they had to cut her out of her vehicle. The man driving the other truck died.

Evelyn is a true child of God and I am asking for your prayers that she recovers from this accident and that her husband and two boys find the strength they need because through the blessing of prayer, we can ask God for help in all kinds of situations, both spiritually and physically.

Sent: Tuesday, June 04, 2013
James and I visited with Russell yesterday afternoon at the hospital. We were able to see her for about five minutes because he knew how close Evelyn and I are to each other. She is still in critical condition. I don't know if she knew I was there, but I rubbed her forehead and talked to her briefly. The doctors are still waiting to get her more stabilized before they can do surgery on her spine area. The bleeding on the brain is not of much concern anymore after looking at the scans. They are more concerned about swelling on her lungs because of the bruises; therefore, they have her on a ventilator to help with her breathing. She has a broken hip, broken femur, and has a broken bone in her lower back. She has a lot of swelling, and as stated yesterday, the next days are crucial. We know that God is in control, and to know Evelyn, we know that she is fighting with everything within her.

Sent: Thursday, June 06, 2013
Russell called and left me a voice mail yesterday afternoon. Things seem to be going a little better. She is breathing a little on her own. She did have surgery Tuesday on her back and her side to

where they put in pins. She will have another surgery today on her hip. She is still heavily sedated. He indicated the doctors may stop the oxidation soon, hoping she may be able to talk at that point. We were in prayer and worship services last night at her church. It was so spiritually uplifting. Everyone had their chance to talk about their experiences with her. They did a video of the service for her to have when she is able to watch it. We as Christians know the power of God and his mighty works; and to Him we give all the honor and glory; for when praises go up, blessings come down. The enemy has come to try and destroy, but God stepped in on time and I feel in my heart He has more work for her to do, which will be in her next book. Please continue to pray for Evelyn because she is like a big sister to me. Will keep you posted as I get updates……Prayer Is A Powerful Weapon.

Sent: Monday, June 10, 2013
Russell called me Friday afternoon. She is still in the trauma unit at McLeod. They tried to wean her off oxidation, but her breathing was too rapid so they put her back on the ventilator. They also tried to back off of the sedation, but her pain tolerance was too high. James and I visited with Evelyn Saturday. When we got to her room, I called her name and she opened her eyes. I just sat and held her hands talking to her and praying. She does have movement of her body and opens/closes her eyes. As far as her recognizing you are there, I do not think she really is aware. But, in spite of what she has gone through and still is going through, I know the angels are still watching over her. I know she is repeating softly some of the lyrics to her latest song, "Liquid Love," that says: 'When I am in need, you are my provider; When I am in battle, you are my victory; and when I am sick, you are my

healer…for my life will never be the same." God's Blessing Is Priceless….

Sent: Monday, June 17, 2013

Friday, James and I visited with Evelyn briefly. She was still sedated, but I felt I wanted to see her. She looked real good. The swelling had gone down a lot and she was beginning to look like herself. I just talked to her and held her hands; James said a prayer and we left. Russell called me while we were on our way there and said he had just left her. He wanted to give me an update. The doctors removed the ventilator (tube going down her throat) from her mouth and put in a tracheotomy. This was done because having a tube going down your throat for a long period of time could possibly affect your vocal cords. The doctors woke her up briefly and put her back to sleep reducing the percentage of the medicine from 50% to 40% and said they would do the same Saturday. Well, To God Be The Glory, Russell called me last night and said the last 24 hours for her were remarkable. They took everything off of her. Yesterday, she was sitting up in bed watching TV and writing notes to him. She does not remember him being there Saturday, what a blessing she is alert. She cannot talk yet, but Russell indicated that the doctors will do something by Wednesday of this week so she will be able to talk. WHAT A MIRACLE.

Now, for the Drayton family, tragedy struck again. They lost their 26-year-old adopted son (John-Michael) Saturday night. He was in a car accident last week and had sustained brain injuries. His funeral is scheduled for Saturday. Evelyn is not aware of this and Russell does not want her to know until she is much stronger. Prayers for this family are much needed.

Sent: Wednesday, June 19, 2013

James and I visited with Evelyn Monday of this week. She was sitting in the chair and writing to us. She looks good. She has no swelling. Her speech therapist was in to see her to put the trach cap on so she will be able to talk. She will have this on for 15 minutes throughout the day. This process strengthens her lungs. Once her lungs are stronger, they will take the large trach tube out and replace it with a small one for a while; from there if her lungs are back to normal, then they will remove the tube and she will be able to talk on her own again. She was so cute – the nurse told her to say something to me and she did. Then she said, but that does not sound like me. The nurse said, but you won't sound like yourself—this is just temporary until you get the trach out, but at least we can understand what you are saying….she just smiled. God is allowing the healing process to continue and to Him, we give all the Glory and Praises because when the praises go up the blessings come down.

Sent: Monday, June 24, 2013

I visited with Evelyn on Saturday. There is nothing much to say other than she is remarkably improving. The large trach tube was taken out and a very small tube replaced it. She sounds like Evelyn now. The nurse even commented to her and said, "Well, you look like you are ready to leave the trauma unit." Even though she has a long recovery ahead of her, she looks good. I did ask her if she remembers the accident – her comment to me was – "Mary, I do not remember anything other than what was told to me – in time, I'm sure God will reveal it back to me." In spite of her downtime, God is still using her to minister – there is a lot to be told. God is dealing with her in a mighty way.

Hallelujah!!! When I left her room, I felt so revived and spiritually lifted. All I can say is that the Power Of God Is Awesome—it just makes me want to get just a little closer to Him because the devil is out to destroy; but we got to know who we are and whose we are. Since her accident, there have already been great blessings and she said there are more to come.

Sent: Monday, July 01, 2013
James and I visited with Evelyn on yesterday. Praise God over and over again for the blessings, the healing, the fellowship and the laughter. We had an awesome visit yesterday. The trach was completely removed and she is talking on her own. Evelyn moved from the ICU ward (she was there for several days) to a regular room on Saturday. Her room number is 1137. She is even on a regular diet now. She is starting to go through therapy. Evelyn looks good. She said listening to what the doctors and nurses told her (bleeding on the brain, broken back, broken hip, broken femur, badly bruised lungs, broken ribs, and pneumonia) she has a lot to give God praises for. A lot of things she did not understand what or why it was happening to her, but they explained to her that all of this is a result of the injuries she sustained from the accident–which she does not remember. But the healing process continues and she is ready to do whatever it takes to have a full recovery. She is so spiritually revived and her whole demeanor is very positive and upbeat. God said that He will never put more on us then we can bear and that He will never leave us or forsake us for He will be our shelter in the time of storm. What a testimony to be told! Thank You Jesus!!!

Wow! I thank Mary for an excellent journal from which I shared several entries. I read the entire journal during my home recuperation. I have relied heavily on her seemingly incredulous notes, along with my medical records, to help me organize my thoughts for this book. I am grateful that my husband gave Mary permission to share medical updates with my former coworkers. Sharing with the coworkers prompted additional prayers for which we are very grateful. Her information is precious to me and continues to uplift me as I occasionally reminisce about my life's journey. I know God blesses those who bless me. With that being said, I pray continued blessings of reciprocity over Mary and James for all their love and support sown into my life. I believe they are continually inspired by my miraculous recovery. Reading Mary's journal makes me want to sing the song "Look Where He Brought Me From" and offer a glorious praise dance at the same time.

Inside Humor: Prior to my accident, about three different people asked me whether Mary was my daughter. I became livid and said, "M*y daughter?*" I was furious because Mary is a year my elder. Can you imagine what other people said *after the accident* when they saw me limping with my cane as Mary and I shopped together? Yep—"*Evelyn, is that your daughter?*" I thought maybe my walking stick and my limping probably added validity to their question this time. Therefore, I decided not to use my cane to trip up the people who made the obnoxious comment. But I told Mary I would not go shopping with her ever again (Ha, ha)! Talking is easy, right? Well, in April 2015, Mary and I went shopping together again in Florence and the store clerk greeted us and said, *"Are you two ladies twins?"* Boy, I felt good and appreciated that status change from being called Mary's mother! Immediately, I told Mary, *"That lady had better be glad she didn't use the word mother in her greeting!"* Mary and I, both donning the same hairstyle, laughed hysterically when we turned the corner. I am so glad to be alive that it doesn't matter what people say! We *shall* go shopping again!

The journal entry about "bleeding on the brain" garners thoughts of the fragility of my mind. While I am not mentally unstable, it still seems Mary had been journalizing the life of another survivor—not about me! Those notes almost compel us to believe death was definitely knocking on my door. The notes also reminded me of an incident prior to my collision when intense fear almost paralyzed me the night I mistakenly thought a prowling cat was a home intruder. The cat prowled through the vinyl underskirting and snarled the duct system of my home. The noise forced me to call the police, but panic sank in when they arrived because I did not hear their vehicle drive up. Listening to the noise surround my house, and then the loud knocking on my door, led me to believe intruders were about to attack me. My heart almost failed as a result of stress and irrational thinking that night. The trauma and dramatization of that night nearly killed me! So I cannot imagine what it would be like for me to have repetitive flashbacks of the nearly deadly vehicle accident I was involved in.

Mary's notes triggered my memory about some things, but I don't recall the initial traumatic moments that took place in my hospital room. As doctors gradually awoke me from the medically induced coma, I saw people in white uniforms looking at me, smiling. I didn't know to call them nurses, but I didn't know that I didn't know. Apparently, I was mentally incapacitated for a short period, but later during my recovery I thought: "Oh, my goodness, what happened to my mind? I am incoherent! I have amnesia!"

Anything's Possible: The 47-Day Prophecy

- I don't remember simple details about myself.
- I don't recall leaving the church I attended in Florence on the day of the accident.
- I don't recall anything that happened at the scene of the accident. **What accident?**
- I don't know which outfit or shoes I wore to church the day of the accident. A photo snapped at the scene shows one shoe on the back seat of my demolished SUV, but I don't recognize the shoe. I guess that shoe belonged to me! Were those the shoes I wore to church or just a spare pair of shoes I left in the vehicle? *I never discovered what was missing from my closet.*
- I don't recall talking to the woman who later identified herself as being the first person at the scene of my accident.
- I don't remember the torrential downpour. I only recall the sun shining brightly earlier the day of the accident, but I am told there was an immense downpour that evening.
- I don't recall the ambulance's flashing lights, the sound of the equipment cutting me from my vehicle, the lifting onto the stretcher, no voices—not anything.
- I don't recall the ambulance trip.
- I don't remember any activity in the emergency room—not to mention the intubation procedure.
- I have no recollection of the actual collision, yet I had to deal with the aftermath of the crash. *Why don't I remember any of this? Is there a medical explanation? I found out that many people lose memory during massive trauma, but* **could it be that God obliterated all of it**

Evelyn Murray Drayton

from my mind because the memory would be too painful?

In a debilitated state of mind, I occasionally responded to touch and sound. I would often hear, "*Hi, Mrs. Drayton.*" However, I could not relate to any communication about an *accident*. I eventually recognized black-and-blue marks all over my body from bruises, torn muscles, and needles, but could not grasp what happened to me. I did not know how to adequately complain to the doctors about anything because I had never experienced such trauma before and did not know what to expect. I did not know what caused my physical abnormalities.

According to Mary Canteen's notes, sometime around mid-June 2013, I was sitting in a chair and writing. I don't have a clue about my first writing attempts. *I was not talking! What happened to my voice? When did I stop talking? What caused the problem?* Records show I entered the hospital with the ability to talk, but something strange happened! I don't know when I lost my speech—or when my speech returned. I did not recall the accident; neither did I recall any pain while I was heavily sedated. My husband indicated I had difficulty swallowing and had not been getting enough air because of my damaged lungs. I thank God for the ventilator that helped to protect, preserve, and prolong my life. I could not breathe without help! Doctors could not elevate my body to drain my punctured lungs because of my broken back. They explained to my husband that a tracheotomy was a vital action to avoid eroding my trachea. The tracheotomy procedure was necessary since I was in a medically induced coma and had already been on a ventilator for an extended period of time. This required doctors to make an incision in my neck that opened an airway to the windpipe—just below the vocal cords. All of this was done to protect my vocal cords and to afford better access to keep my lungs clear of fluid. The surgery also aimed to defend my body from infections due to extended use of my breathing tube. Unfortunately, the infection risk was high and I did contract pneumonia.

The extended ventilator usage led to my need for a speaking device, which was a valve put on the tracheotomy that allowed me to talk. I was assigned a speech therapist at McLeod Medical Center who treated me with the utmost care. She was very friendly and prepared for me a dish of *blue* peach cobbler and called it *"smurf."* I thought, *"Why in the world is this cobbler not yellow?"* That cobbler was really a part of the therapist's treatment to determine my ability to swallow after the tracheotomy. That *smurf* did not look palatable, but it was necessary at the time. I wanted to talk again, so I looked at that *smurf*, closed my eyes, and gulped it down. The therapist was so proud of me. As I recovered and no longer needed ventilator support, the tracheotomy tube was removed. My husband said he does not recall the first word I said to him when my voice returned a few days later—but it was a blessing to hear me speak again. He said I incomprehensibly told him that I had heard about **his** terrible accident. *Why didn't I realize that I was in the bed suffering and not my husband?* My mind continued to play tricks with me as my voice improved. My voice returned and the stoma left from the tracheotomy healed in a timely manner. Now I seem to take advantage of every opportunity to open my mouth and talk. I am so grateful!

The medical staff treated me like I was a *celebrity*! I thought to myself, *Wow! What did I do to deserve all of this attention?* Even though my speech was returning, my mind was still wandering. There were days I questioned whether I had died and would rub my face or other body part just to be sure I was still alive. Even then I was not sure! I recall a nurse said, *"Mrs. Drayton, I am so sorry about your accident, but I am so glad you are here. You are such an encouragement and such a blessing to us."* **Where was here?** *Was I at work?* **Was it Heaven?** I didn't know I was in a hospital! I also recall during a shift change another nurse hugged me and said, *"Mrs. Drayton, you sound so good. This is the first time I've heard you **talk** since you were **here**. It's so good to hear your beautiful* *voice."* I don't know my verbal response, but I thought, *"How come she's never heard me **talk here** before?"* I don't have a clue what I possibly could have said to be an encouragement and a blessing to them. If only those nurses knew how their words helped to change *my* mind and my life.

I experienced and endured the constant needles piercing my skin. I even endured the hallucinations, whether from medication or the brain injury, I do not know. I had read something somewhere about left brain and right brain activities due to trauma, but I could not pinpoint which side was doing what. This sounds weird, but I was not asleep at the time this happened: my medical equipment became social media outlets. My intravenous (IV) equipment served me as a radio, a telephone, and even a computer screen—depending on what my thoughts were and whatever I needed the equipment to be at the time. I even asked a nurse to catch the phone for me one time. I experienced real-life events in hearing the phone ring and answering the phone. I cannot explain how that happened, but my husband will attest that *I left a message on a specific party's answering service asking the party to return my call to my **home** number. The person called the house and informed my husband I had left a message to call the house. Did a nurse assist me with the call?* **How did I remember the telephone number when I didn't even know my pelvis was broken—when I didn't even know I was in the hospital?** I asked the party to call the house and I left the correct number for the party to call. **How did that happen? I must have had an angel beside me!**

One of the nurses told me that I was in the hospital and asked if I knew the hospital name. I don't recall at what point of my recovery that this hospital name questioning session began, but I recall her saying, *"No,"* several different times. I could not figure out *why* the nurse said I was in a hospital. On one occasion, I told a nurse I was at MUSC in Andrews, South Carolina, and she again said, **"*No.*"** I felt the nurses were tricking me because I just **knew** I was right—ha, ha. Well, Andrews doesn't even have a hospital, but I dreamt it did! The city of Andrews popped up again and again! In spite of all the questioning, it did not occur to me that I was bedridden. It seemed I was in an office at work and I informed a nurse who I thought was my coworker: *"I'm going to leave Andrews and run to Georgetown to get my hair fixed. I'll be right back."* The nurse played along with me and said, *"We don't want you to go today, Mrs. Drayton."* I wondered, *"Why not today?"* I don't know why the town of Andrews lingered in my mind. Pray for me because I still don't know why.

  Nearly a month had gone by before I actually understood that I was hospitalized and could finally memorize the name *McLeod*. I didn't know I was at McLeod Regional Medical Center in Florence. For the people who didn't know me or my condition, they could have easily thought I was totally inebriated. After my release from the hospital, I laughed when I saw pictures of my pillow emblazoned with the name **McLeod Regional Medical Center**. Why didn't I respond to the nurse correctly and say, *"McLeod?"* Better yet, why didn't they show me a pillowcase and ask me to read it? Maybe they did show me some things with the hospital name and I didn't understand. I was sleeping on the hospital name—and didn't know it! I know the hospital name was neatly etched on other items in my room, but I didn't know. I thank God daily for restoring my mental competence.

  The same **Shirley Davis** who informed my husband about my accident came to visit me while I was still in the trauma unit. She told me she had visited prior to this day, but I had been comatose for an extended period. It seems like Shirley told me that I was in a bad wreck and that *I hit somebody* with my vehicle. The truth is someone actually hit me, but I didn't know that at the time! There were no family members in my room when Shirley arrived and I didn't have a clue what she was talking about because I did not recall being in a collision. Shirley's daughter, I believe, showed me a picture of my damaged vehicle.

Looking at the picture, one might easily conclude that my vehicle had caused the accident. I requested that her daughter send a copy of the photo to my email that she supposedly entered into her cell phone. I never received the email from her so I assumed she erroneously entered my email on her telephone. I wrote my correct email on the same paper, on which Shirley wrote her name, address, and telephone number and gave to me. *How did I remember an email address?* **When was I capable of doing all of this in the trauma unit?** I have no explanation about the timing or my health condition at the time of this visit. Since I don't know the date of Shirley's visit, I cannot honestly say what happened first or next. But it is puzzling that I did not remember a discussion with Shirley about the accident until after my hospital release. *Why do I vaguely recall parts of Shirley's conversation now, but not then?* I cannot explain how I communicated well enough to write, talk, and spell correctly. I am baffled how all of this happened! *Did Shirley's alarming news cause me to relapse?* Was it the medication or stress from the news about the accident? According to my medical log, one day I started asking the nurses senseless questions. These could have been triggered subliminal messages from visitors conversing in my room—I just don't know. *Who preserved the handwritten note to ensure it was not trashed? Did I request someone secure the paper for me?* **This was not a dream**—I have the original paper with Shirley's handwriting **AND MINE!** I mailed a copy of the paper to Shirley in May 2015 and thanked her for allowing God to use her to bless my family and me. To prove the address was valid, I asked Shirley to mail a response to me and I still have her stamped reply envelope in my possession.

During the period that I could not talk, I resorted to writing. I thought I was writing complete sentences, and even paragraphs. I wrote a note to one of my young relatives and he made a gesture with his hand and then made this vocal response: *"Evelyn, I'll be glad when you get out of this hospital so you can read your writing."* My writing seemed to be written perfectly in my own eyes. The way he looked at the paper, I concluded he couldn't pronounce the words. Rolling my eyes and panting profusely, I murmured: "*I thought that boy could read better than that!*" Even with bleeding on my brain and frequent heavy sedation, the Holy Spirit still ministered to me saying: "*You looked at him and said he can't read, but you did not look at yourself and say you could not write.*" Within my own mind, I *could* write plainly, so what was Holy Spirit saying to me? I was guilty of being too judgmental and had to repent! I did not know that the poorly written note I gave the young man consisted of gibberish—only lines and circles. A few days after that note-writing episode, though, I wrote complete sentences, but I had a lot of misspelled words at first. AND I have learned not to be judgmental by decrying others without first looking at myself. WOW!

> "*Thou hypocrite, first cast out the beam out of thine own eye: and then thou shalt see clearly to cast out the mote out of thy brother's eye*" (Matthew 7:5).

Not being fully aware of my surroundings or health status, I capitalized on the bits and pieces as best I could. I struggled with my cognitive skills, but I did not allow this to impede my overall recovery. Visitors continually stopped by my room, although I could not plainly converse with them—and in some instances, could not identify them. My son, Justin, served as my interpreter and a friendly intermediary while my voice was clearing. It was only my imagination that he sat on my hospital bed with his back propped against the wall, caring for me and handling my needs. My vocabulary was limited and I would often think one thing, but say another. I recalled an incident where I thought my SUV was parked at a shopping center, not in the hospital parking lot. So I asked my husband to run and get my cell phone from the SUV. I did not remember the accident; and, therefore, did not know my SUV was destroyed. If I recall correctly, my husband told me my vehicle was not outside. Was that statement a ploy to avoid the long hike to my vehicle? How could I suggest the location of a cell phone and not know the difference between a shopping center and a hospital? Knowing myself, I believe I presented more questions to him, but I don't recall the follow-up questions.

My eldest sister, **Junetta Smith** (aka Juanita), is so sweet and wears a beautiful smile! She and her husband, **Benita,** drove from Orlando, Florida, to be with me. I don't recall a lot of details about their visit, but I wanted to go to lunch with my sister. I was still being fed intravenously, but I didn't know it. The nurse told me I couldn't go to lunch, but that my sister could bring me something to eat. I told the nurse that the restaurant was just around the corner and that we would be right back. Again, I didn't know that I was incapacitated. I was a little upset with the nurse, but I accepted her negative response. I cannot imagine what was going through that nurse's mind when I made such a request while bedridden. At the time, I did not know that I could not walk or that needles and tubes impaled my frail body. Later, it seems I was mesmerized by my sister's makeup and her colorful attire. I complimented her for choosing the wine-colored shade of lipstick. Afterward, I told her my lips needed some moisture and that her lipstick would also make me look pretty. The nurse reentered my room soon after I applied the lipstick and said, *"Mrs. Drayton, you look pretty wearing that lipstick!"* I think the nurse redeemed herself from my wrath after those kind words. I don't think I had looked in a mirror during my entire hospital stay, and if I did, I don't remember it. Instead of using a mirror, I warmly accepted the nurse's compliment and agreed with her good judgment call! I wonder if my sister discarded her tube of lipstick after I smeared it on my chapped lips. If she tossed it, I certainly understand. Love you, Sis!

You may think I had already suffered through my trauma and had rebounded, but near my fourth week in the hospital, I faced an emotional challenge. My husband walked into my room one day and told me that he needed to share something with me, but I interrupted, saying, *"I don't want anything to disrupt my peace."* After my interruption, he chose to watch the television with me instead of holding a discussion. It was evident that something unusual was going on, but I was ambivalent about his purpose. I thought maybe he had found himself another woman. No, that was not medication talking that was my insecurity after being away from my husband for such a long time. After all, on the day of the accident, I told him I would drive over to Florence and would return home within a few hours—those hours evolved into weeks.

Upon Russell's visit the following day, I asked him to pull a chair directly facing me and talk to me about yesterday's intended discussion. I remembered! I thought we would discuss his Fourth of July celebration plans—and end the discussion about some of my unpaid bills! Instead, he assured me that he loved me and that he had some news to share with me. He recited the names of several people from the community who had died while I was hospitalized. Then he showed me two obituaries which I thought were for two of the elderly people he mentioned. Surprisingly, the first one was the face of a young, light-skinned handsome man that I had never seen before; I had never even heard the name before. Russell explained that he was the young man involved in my vehicle accident and was killed at the scene. It was still hard for me to comprehend that I was involved in an accident—I didn't remember it. This was definitely the first time I had ever heard that someone died from the accident in which I was involved. Did I kill the man? Did he try to kill me? I didn't understand at first.

Lastly, Russell told me to flip to the second obituary. He had strategically planned this last obituary for discussion. You see, I had just made it through the acute phase of trauma to the step-down trauma unit and there I was looking at the obituary for **John-Michael Drayton**, our nephew. John is the young man that Russell and I reared as a son from the age of 12, now age 26. John was killed in a vehicle accident and was already eulogized and buried nearly two weeks before anyone could inform me. My husband gently shared the news with me, but extreme mental trauma about it escaped me. My stoic facial features probably remained the same because God had already prepared me to receive the sad news. It seems so surreal that John-Michael was dead! News about John's death and the funeral were held in silence for fear of me having a relapse after suffering my brain hemorrhage. Russell said he feared losing me and wanted to spare me the grief over John's death. Yet he yielded and told me only because he didn't want me to find out from another source. Russell, being under a lot of pressure, handled the conversation considerably well. Russell had entertained family gatherings at our home in remembrance of John, referred to as *sitting up* or *wake*. Family members and community residents jointly provided food and drinks to accommodate the crowd. He said all of the deaths he mentioned occurred within days of each other and that he had attended a few of the funeral services. I cannot imagine what my husband was going through after losing his nephew and dealing with his wife barely gliding through the fatality statistics.

    The sad news about John lingered in my heart and on my mind, but God has a way that is mighty sweet. Cautiously, God had strengthened my heart that day to accept the grievous news. You see, I had already dreamt that my friend's son was killed. I had already cried and grieved during the night for her and her loss. It had become clear why I shed all those tears in my dream. My heart was being prepared to handle the news about John. I reflected on some of the times I had fussed with John about cleaning his room. I also smiled about the shared laughter when John told me that my husband and I kiss like characters from *Planet of the Apes*. But, most importantly, I thought of our last telephone conversation when John told me how much he loved me. God kept me emotionally stable throughout this trauma and I am eternally grateful. No matter how people describe the tragedy, I know the details I saw in my dream! John—gone but not forgotten!

Ironically, the same night John-Michael died someone hacked my email account and sent various vulgar messages and links to all of my email contacts. I guess I will never know who sent the email or why it happened on this same night. I know that I did not send the email because I was just being weaned from a ventilator in the hospital on that email date. I did not know about the computer violation and probably would not have known without my friend's apologetic remark for being unable to open the link that I sent her. I asked her what email she was talking about. After my hospital release, I deleted all the bulk distribution except one of the emails remains in my account only to confirm the date of the email blast.

Although I did not talk a lot about my mental healing, it was absolutely phenomenal how God kept a word in my heart. I prayed and thought on words from the Bible that I had memorized to gain knowledge, strength, and support to deal with my emotional and mental setback. I don't recall my first laugh after the accident. However, I know my hospital occupational therapists were usually attractive young men and women who often complimented me—and I know they made me smile—or laugh! The therapists challenged me with different strategies to improve my memory and coordination problems; they noted that I was progressing remarkably well.

I was progressing well, but I still had a long way to go with my thought process. At one point, when the nurses removed stitches from my face, I told them, *"Don't mess up my eyebrow arch!"*—I thought I was in a beauty salon. In response, I recall hearing the words *"terrible accident,"* but even then I did not fully understand that I had a near-death experience. For several weeks I intermittently comprehended being in a hospital. Most of my visitors appeared to have met me in a conference room, not in a hospital room. It seems I also visited the library and several different restaurants. I don't recall ever eating in the restaurants, but there were people I recognized or had conversations with in restaurants. A combination of the head injury and the strong medication had me somewhat mentally incapacitated. I tried to watch television and read through magazines, but I did not comprehend well. For a while, television was only *noise with pictures*. The emergency room report indicated that I appeared alert upon arrival. However, supplementary medical reports indicate that I didn't comprehend being in an accident. I had a hard time keeping a single thought in my head. I always saw myself being busy and productive, not lying in a hospital bed. It seems I was an employee at a library and spent time working on the computer, continuously striving to complete a project before going home. On one occasion, it seems everyone had vacated the library except me, and security personnel locked me inside. I don't recall how or if I ever got home from the library.

The morphine had me so agitated and delusional at times that I made several attempts to get out of my bed. I recall trying to sneak out of bed to use the restroom, not knowing I couldn't get up, even if someone had paid me to do so. In my mind, it seems I wanted to tiptoe to the restroom—just to see if I could sneak without getting caught! So I kept trying to roll to the edge of the bed. The nurse caught me trying to roll one time and asked me what I was trying to do. And like a child, I disingenuously said, "*Nothing!*" Maybe that was a hallucination, but the nurse made notes in my medical records to reflect my devious attempt to get out of bed. I just cannot confirm it was the same day in question or whether I tried this on other days as well. Oh goodness, I gave those nurses a hard time!

Nurses awoke me at different hours of the night for my new health improvement regiment and routine breathing treatments. To help clear and strengthen my lungs, I was administered medication through a breathing apparatus that, in my opinion, mimicked a person smoking a peace pipe. Whenever I exhaled, steam filled the air as if I had puffed smoke. It seemed to me that I was being trained how to properly manage my hand while smoking—instead of learning how to breathe. Just for the fun of it, I held the pipelike apparatus and stuck my little pinky finger out to the side to see what it looked like if I were a smoker. *How did I know to pretend I was smoking and enjoy the sarcasm?* That circulation of steam to simulate smoking was too much drama and work for me—that acting session lasted only a few minutes. The appearance of smoking a pipe or a cigarette was not ladylike for me and became less appealing. Consequently, I eventually asked the nurse if she would let me try a different breathing equipment style, which she gladly obliged. I was supposed to be in pain and having a pity party over my injuries—but praise God—I still had joy!

Reverend Dr. Melton Johnson and his lovely wife, **First Lady Margaree Pearson Johnson**, one of my relatives, drove all the way from Roanoke, Virginia, to visit me. While they were in my room, I was so discombobulated. They could readily find my clean and soiled tissues hidden everywhere. Sister Margaree said jokingly, *"Evelyn, you are just squirreling away tissue!"* In just a short while, she and her husband went to the store to purchase a pouch for me to store my clean tissue and personal items. They also bought me some lotion to help clear the dark bruises on my body. It blessed me to know they drove so far to check on me and offer assistance to me. What a blessing! A few years earlier they had invited me to be their guest speaker at historical First Baptist Church in Salem, Virginia. Their hospitality was second to none!

My friend, Mary Canteen, continued to make frequent visits at the hospital. She purchased a manicure set for me, trimmed my nails, and massaged my legs and feet using the lotion Sister Margaree had purchased. This was spa treatment at its best! I meticulously checked my scribbled notes and concluded that John-Michael's funeral was held the same day Mary showed all of this kindness to me. This could have been a small matter to her, but it meant the world to me when my mind cleared. It is amazing how small, loving acts of kindness can mean so much to those who need it.

> *"I have shewed you all things, how that so labouring ye ought to support the weak, and to remember the words of the Lord Jesus, how he said, It is more blessed to give than to receive"* (Acts 20:35).

After much loving care and medical treatment, I was recovering nicely. The doctor ordered that I sit up several times a day using a back brace each time I got out of bed. I thought, *"This bed feels good, but I wonder if that chair is comfortable too."* I didn't know my spine and pelvis were broken and that I needed a lumbar brace to get to the chair. I vaguely recall some pain on the day a man fitted me for a back brace, but I did not know what they were doing to me at the time. I didn't know anything about a back brace! I thought the young man who measured me for my back brace owned a company in Andrews and was one of comedian Chris Rock's brothers. **I don't have a clue where that idea came from!** The man blushed as if he was honored and enjoyed the idea of being related to Chris Rock. I blushed because I thought I was correct! (Don't laugh but, frankly, upon my release from the hospital, I searched the Andrews telephone book to call the company and thank the brother for his service.) It was just a figment of my imagination that Chris Rock has a brother with a company located in Andrews. What an illusion! After the measuring procedure was completed, the nurse told me, *"You did a good job, Mrs. Drayton!"* I really didn't know what was going on.

It was funny how specially trained people came and taught the nurses and me how I would be lifted and transported from my bed to the chair—wearing my new back brace, of course. I did not fully realize I was incapacitated. I was shocked when I discovered my condition. Frustration overtook me the very first day when the nurses actually followed the doctor's order to get me

Anything's Possible: The 47-Day Prophecy

out of bed. The nurses hooked me up and snapped a contraption between my legs as if I were in a baby carriage.

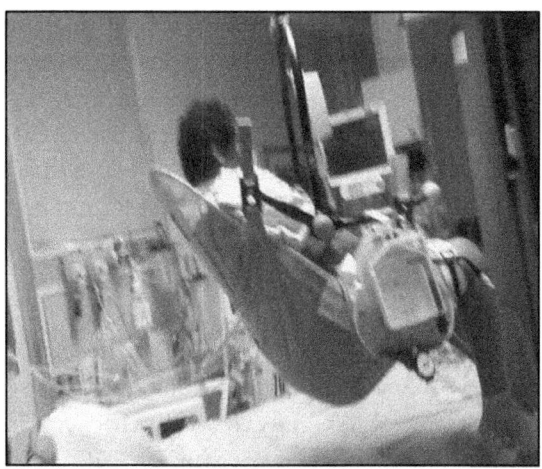

Out of the coma! Up, up, and away to my chair!

With the press of buttons, the carriage lifted me from my bed to the chair. I was once this fast-walking inspirational speaker and there I was in midair, swinging on this apparatus. I looked like a cartoon character as I was lifted from my bed. Ironically, my friend, Mary Canteen, snapped a picture of this *comical* moment. Mary said she felt sorrow and joy to witness that moment, knowing I had been in a prolonged coma. At the same time she was tickled to see me in such a precarious—and hilarious—position.

One day, as a nurse prepared me to be lifted from bed, the carriage accidently bumped my damaged knee. It was such an excruciating pain! I told the nurse, *"I don't want to wear that old back brace anymore. Besides, you hurt my knee really bad, so I will report you to my attorney."* The nurse said, *"You want me to hand you the telephone to report it?"* My curt response was simply, *"Uh-uh. No, ma'am."* She called my bluff! Why was I so mean? My voice had returned, so I should have been an absolute sweetheart! Right!

I detested wearing that back brace and I believe that best encapsulates my feelings about that contraption. The brace surrounded my abdomen which caused discomfort due to pressure on the stomach feeding tube. There was also an upper piece of the back brace that interfered with the tracheal tube. There was a great deal of discomfort, but after much complaining, some slight adjustments were made to the brace. I engineered the brace by inserting a towel between the tracheal tube and the back brace, which gave me a little relief. Regardless of the adjustments, I continued to vent my frustration and told a nurse, who was pregnant, "*If you put that back brace on me one more time, I am going to sue you.*" That nurse—without cracking a smile—wrapped the back brace around me as if she was tightly sealing it over my lips. Even with my righteous bravado, I couldn't bluff my way out of that one! The nurse was only trying to help me! **Why was I so grumpy? How do I remember this detail?** The medication probably had me agitated! Plus, I didn't like that back brace—can't you tell? When the shift changed, I told some of the other nurses, "*I don't want to get out of bed just to sit in a chair for hours. I'll just stay in bed.*" I felt like saying, "*You're not the boss of me to make me get out of bed.*"*(Ha, ha!)* The nurses had to follow the doctor's orders, so you know I had to get up, right? There was a lot of pain associated with wearing that back brace, but *I still did not comprehend my back was broken.* Initially, I was angry with the nurses, but became submissive when they presented the danger of not wearing the brace to protect my broken back. When all the dust settled, I ended up willingly wearing the back brace with no further complaints. I know I had a bad attitude toward those nurses for several days. I recall apologizing for not being a good patient. I know those nurses have many humorous stories to tell among all their stories of pain and sorrow they witness on a daily basis. The tenacity of those nurses made me a better woman—they refused to let me win the fight. The battle was for my own good so I, too, am now a woman of tenacity and drive. When I understood my situation, it was an honor to know that I was still alive and finally able to sit in a chair with a back brace, realizing I could have been paralyzed—or dead. That back brace prevented me from becoming paralyzed and I didn't even know it. Sometimes, it seems, we don't want the things that are good for us.

Records indicate that I was steadily improving and it was time to move to another level in my rehabilitative process. I had already endured being on life support, using a ventilator to help me breathe, and using a feeding tube to help with my nutrition. My condition had been so severe that doctors placed me in a medically induced coma to allow my body to heal. At the appropriate time doctors woke me from the coma when my condition improved. To get me to the next level of improvement, McLeod's in-house physical therapy was given charge to provide extensive strengthening to enable me to independently sit, stand, and move around—and also to help me with swallowing and breathing. I had a weight-bearing restriction on my left leg and could only put weight on my right leg for a short period at first. A therapist was assigned to help me maneuver from my bed, without any lifting equipment, and teach me how to pivot. He had me dancing on one foot—and that foot was on top the therapist's feet as he taught me to stand and pivot. I began to pivot from my bed to the chair—no more baby-carriage lifting for me! I told my husband on his next visit, *"If you hear that I was dancing with another man, he was only my therapist who was teaching me how to walk."* A visitor laughed that I even bothered to explain the **dancing with another man** to my husband, with my broken hip and wearing a back brace around my body! (I laugh at myself now just to think about it!) Records also indicate that I steadily became more independent, even to the point of being *bossy*. The staff said they liked that about me!

One day I noticed a piece of new equipment delivered to my room—a bedside potty! Though I flittered with my independence, the first time the nurse told me to try getting out of bed to use the potty, I said, *"Do what?"* I was spoiled rotten by now with all the loving care and just squeezing my red button for a nurse! It seems I was still connected to tubes and I did not want to graduate from my catheter and bedpan. I fought the urge to be rude, so I learned the masterful skill of getting out of bed for potty breaks.

    After teaching me to pivot with minimal assistance, the therapist introduced me to my first wheelchair spin. I had a hard time steering at first, so they watched me meander down the hallway. Over time I became an expert wheelchair driver—in my opinion! By this time I had learned to stand on my good leg beside my bed with minimal assistance. One day I wheeled myself to the gym for physical therapy. I was hesitant in performing my recommended therapy routine, but as I sat there contemplating *if* I wanted to exercise, a nurse wheeled in a young one-legged man. When I noticed the missing leg, I immediately and speedily lifted my legs high in praise and thanksgiving for being alive with two legs. I was moving my injured leg so fast, the nurse told me, *"Take it easy, Mrs. Drayton!"* Sometimes we need to understand that our situation may be bad, but it could be considerably worse. While I was still exercising my legs, I observed the young man's ill-mannered behavior toward the therapist. As I watched and listened to the young man, though, I had to hold my tongue. I was about to scold him for being very arrogant and verbally disrespectful to his friendly and strict disciplinarian therapist. This therapy session humbled me as I thought about my own behavior related to my back brace and felt the urge to repent. I am grateful that I still have two legs and feet with toes to lift. Just like the impotent man in the Bible who could not walk, Jesus told him to take up his mat and walk (John 5). Though things felt a little discouraging at one point, I lifted my head high and declared, *"The same way that I started talking and writing, one day I will walk again."* Though I fatigued easily, I had a relentless endurance to hold on to my faith and my healing. I also yearned to see the young man change his behavior and give respect to those who diligently give of themselves to help others.

I agreed with the doctors when they said *"therapy served me well."* My physical and occupational therapy sessions were very effective. I overheard some visitors inquiring about my room number as they approached the nurse's station. They were actually bypassing my room, but I whistled with a *"psst, psst"* sound to get their attention. They were surprised to see me sitting comfortably in a chair instead of lying in a bed. Those visitors reportedly said, based on rumors in the community, they came with expectations of seeing my arms and legs suspended in midair. They did not determine the veracity of the rumors, so they looked at me in disbelief that I had recovered so nicely and had exceeded their expectations. Several other people told me they visited me when I was in the coma, but neither my husband nor I knew they visited until they revealed it months later, after I returned home. One friend told me that he and his wife visited me and began to pray. He said as he laid his hand over me to pray, the power of the Holy Spirit resonated from my body and lifted his hand. He then heard the Holy Spirit speak to him and said, *"She will be all right."* He was assured that *"I shall not die, but live, and declare the works of the Lord"* (Psalm 118:17).

As my condition improved, it was a blessing to be stepped down from the trauma unit to a regular room. The night I moved from the trauma unit was the same night I received my first hot meal since being hospitalized. **I thought someone was throwing me a party for sure!** One of the first things I requested when I moved to my regular room was a head massage! ***A head massage?!*** A nurse put a warm cap on my head and granted my request. The nurse very carefully massaged my head, granting me extreme pleasure and comfort. She also gave me a nice, warm full-body bath and that felt wonderful. Those nurses treated me like a queen this first night in my new room. And to top that, I was blessed to have my husband spend the night by my side—**well, *he was there beside my feet!***

I don't know how many days I stayed in that room before they transferred me to the orthopedic section where a long bar extended over my bed. My mind was set to recover and restore my health by all means necessary. So, when I noticed the bar, I just ***assumed*** this was the room where my intensive physical therapy sessions would be conducted. Stupidly, I immediately tested my strength as I reached up to grab the bar—without wearing my back brace. **Yes, I did—I reached up and grabbed the bar!** Oh, for the mercy of God! Oh, only for the grace of our God I was not injured! I could have pulled my back out of place and paralyzed myself while *in* the hospital. **Neither you nor I know the totality of what could have happened!** Oh, my God—after all of that in-house therapy—just look at what I did! I should have known better! Satan tried different tactics to destroy me. If it were not for God's mercy I would not be alive today. **God covered me!**

Several days later, nearing the end of my hospital stay, the doctors tested me and quarantined my room due to my high fever and questionable frequent bodily excretions. The doctors were baffled about this latest development and sent biopsies to the Centers for Disease Control. Even the food service personnel were not allowed in my room; they left my food outside my door, and my nurses wore masks to deliver my meals. This was a very disheartening time. I believe there was a mistaken duplicate dose of medication which led to this situation—just as I had dreamt earlier. I had actually shared my dream of the medication mix-up before it happened, but one of the nurses said I just needed some rest. Nevertheless, I had no medical expertise to challenge the nurses' records or the doctors' orders. Through it all, I had to look forward, not backward.

I eventually recovered and a few days later the doctors were contemplating releasing me from the hospital. Doctors opined that I was ready for advance rehabilitative treatment. However, I was vacillating between going home and transferring to a rehabilitation facility. Amidst the discussions, I was experiencing intense restlessness as doctors reduced my pain medication dosage, but I managed the discomfort by utilizing about five pillows just to get a good night's rest. I still had the feeding tube in my stomach as doctors were making plans to release me. My primary physician finally ordered the removal of my stomach peg. The nurse on duty told me she had never removed a stomach peg before and didn't want mine to be her first removal after all I had been through. She called the doctor about her reservation, so the doctor came the next day and yanked it out. It was quick and a little painful, but at least it was out. I told the doctor I was expecting him to sedate me before he pulled that stomach peg. He had the audacity to say, *"Why would I do that?"* then hurriedly turned away and continued to look at some of my medical papers. My exact thought: *"Well, duh…to spare me the pain, sir!"* I wanted to be livid, but I smiled instead. I guess the doctor laughed inwardly to witness me tolerating all the other excruciating pain then squirming over the little pinch from the peg removal! As the incision healed, the nurse referred to the scar as my second navel!

There was not a legitimate reason to repine my return home in a wheelchair. Therefore, when the support staff and my doctor conferred with me, I was adamant about returning home. I asserted my authority and chose to go home instead of rehab. They prepared all the paperwork accordingly and I was ready to hit the road. Naturally, I was appalled when my husband disagreed. Several thoughts crossed my mind: *Maybe my broken body and my uncombed hair had me looking too tired and disheveled to go home. Maybe he doesn't want to be married to me anymore. Maybe he has a girlfriend.* Russell assured me of his love and told me that going to rehab would benefit both him and me. I honored his tenacity through the entire ordeal, but still debated because I have a tendency to vacillate when important decisions need to be made. My friends, James and Mary Canteen, entered my room just as Russell and I were discussing the matter. Mary shared how rehab benefited her brother and how it would help me as well. Both James and Mary agreed with Russell and persuaded me to go to rehab. Ultimately, the final choice was mine, and I concurred with the majority, which turned out to be one of the best decisions I ever made. Although Russell himself was treated at the emergency room for headaches during my hospitalization, he remained a pillar of strength. Through his unwavering support, I vicariously lived the life of a strong woman, though my body and mind were frail.

I made the final decision to transfer to rehab instead of returning home for recovery. Yet in the back of my mind I was still shouting: *I WANT TO GO HOME NOW!* On the other hand, I tried to figure out how I would cope with the new environment at rehab. How will I handle myself? How are the people going to treat me? What is God going to do with me at rehab? Was I apprehensive? Yes, you bet I was. I didn't know what to expect. I didn't know what people do or how they behave at rehab centers. Questions, unspoken scenarios, and more questions rattled my fragile mind!

HealthSouth Rehabilitation Center

After my extended stay at McLeod Regional Health Center, I finally transferred *across the street* to HealthSouth Rehabilitation Center, where doctors scheduled me to remain about two weeks. I missed being at McLeod, but had brought along fond memories. I was able to reflect upon and compare the exceptional care rendered by the amazing team of doctors, nurses, occupational and physical therapists, and all the support personnel. I even reflected upon those who gave encouraging words as they mopped my floor and cleaned my room.

My expectation of ill treatment at HealthSouth was prominent on my radar screen since I had witnessed a patient mistreated at *an old folks' nursing home*. Astonishingly, my first week of rehabilitation at HealthSouth was exciting. The primary physician at this facility said I had suffered a lot and must have had angels flying over me to have survived such a tragic accident. He called me *"Church Lady."*

This doctor was so pleasant and I always looked forward to chatting with him. He ordered a battery of tests to evaluate my speech and my mental and physical statuses. I made up my mind that I would make the best of the transition and prepare myself to work hard. I wanted to learn tips on how to cope with my injuries and care for myself once I got home.

HealthSouth served timely and delicious meals. My teeth were extremely sensitive, but I reluctantly ate and drank according to schedule. I was excited that Russell and Nicholas visited and actually spent the very first Sunday night with me at rehab. I enjoyed their presence and the fellowship. It reminded me of being home with them. I did not even have to take sleeping pills that night because I was so peaceful. So far so good!

After a restful weekend, it was time to hit the gym. I was proud to wear the casual clothing that my amazing friend, Mary Canteen, purchased for me to wear to my therapy sessions. She stepped up to the plate again and provided whatever she noticed I was lacking. I know Russell appreciated the loyal support that Mary, from a woman's point of view, offered to me. I went to physical therapy as scheduled while wheelchair-bound, hoping I would leave the facility walking on two feet. My therapists at McLeod had already trained me how to pivot using my right foot. To my disappointment, the doctor ordered zero weight-bearing tolerance for that broken left leg. My weight-bearing status never changed while at HealthSouth, so I was limited to pivoting on my right leg only. The remarkable part about this situation was that my right leg also suffered bruised and torn muscles and was immensely painful. Yet the doctor referred to this leg as my *"good leg"* because it escaped broken bones. What a laugh! The right leg was more painful than the broken left leg! Although I was temporarily limited to a non-weight-bearing state and my training was restricted, there were many other things I could learn to do other than learning how to walk again. My confidence level increased as I learned new skills in the training, waiting, and healing process. As HealthSouth therapists continued to remediate my physical impairments, I tried to maintain a good attitude and gave the utmost respect to them and their instructions. I steered my wheelchair, lifted my legs, and completed all the other challenges required of me. I completed my tasks as if I was totally healed, and I know God encouraged me so that I could look forward to the challenging days ahead.

Sporadically, my body made major adjustments to the physical conditioning from the gym exercise routine. The excruciating pain forced me to mumble to myself, *"I'm **not** going back to therapy!"* Then I remembered that in order to go home I had better go back to therapy sessions! So that scenario was speedily rectified. Period! Also, keep in mind that the stomach peg was recently removed and my pain medication dosages had been drastically reduced. These changes did not work in my favor. The pulses of pain became so intolerable that I wished I was anesthetized; but, since I was alert, my request for both sleeping pills and painkillers was granted.

As I boarded the elevator one day after therapy, Shirley Davis, the lady who informed my husband about my accident, stepped on also. I didn't have a clue who this woman was—she could have been anybody. As a matter of fact, she, along with her son, followed me to my room and asked me if I knew who she was. She looked at me as if I should have known her, but I didn't. I couldn't think of a family member she resembled, so I admitted I didn't know her. She told me she had visited me before and then reintroduced herself and her son. As she talked to me, I vaguely recalled a woman telling me that *I had hit someone with my vehicle.* Police records confirmed, though, that someone had actually hit my vehicle. The first time Shirley visited me, I was in intensive care and no family members were present. Again, none of my relatives were in my room this time either, only this strange woman and her son. I believe the Holy Spirit told me to *hold my peace.* Therefore, I did not tell her that my husband had received an official police report about the accident. Neither did I disclose that my memory of her visit to the trauma unit had vaguely returned. I didn't know if she concluded that I had hit the other party based on the condition of the vehicles. I didn't know if the young man who died was her relative and she was upset with me because he died. Was this woman upset with me? I just didn't know how to handle this predicament! With so many things happening those days, I just didn't know what to think with these two strangers in my room!

Suddenly, Shirley shared that her son had accepted Jesus Christ into his life and received salvation since her last visit. I was intrigued by that announcement and offered words of encouragement to both of them. Before they left my room, Shirley gave me an original poem she penned and placed it in a beautiful frame just for me. I read the poem aloud several times and asked her to sign the back, giving me permission to include the poem in a book someday. She consented and was proud that I was enthralled by her work.

This is the beautiful poetry that Shirley Davis granted to me, titled *This Is How God Made Me*:

This Is How God Made Me

This is how God made me
To think, feel, see, hope, and believe in the impossible.
You see this is how God made me
To see a full course meal when I think the cupboard is bare.
You see this is how God made me
To move hills and mountains while kneeling on my knees.
You see this is how God made me
To try reaching for the sky although I know my arms and hands are too short.
You see this is how God made me
To step out on faith even when I cannot feel or see.
You see this is how God made me
To stand still while the wind is blowing in different directions

Evelyn Murray Drayton

You see this is how God made me
To give my enemies the best I have and still have some for my friends.
You see this is how God made me
To step out on faith when it seems like all hope is gone.
You see this is how God made me
To walk with my head held high and not stumble or fall.
You see this is how God made me
To find the warmth of God's love even when there is no fire.
You see this is how God made me
To mend a broken spirit without any splints.
You see this is how God made me
Not to let lies pierce my heart.
*You take the **L** to love, **I** to increase, **E** to endure, and **S** to seal my faith.*
You see this is how God made me. What about you?
****

I had lain upon my bed many days anticipating the day I would get up without assistance—and it finally happened. One day I paged my nurse to help me to the potty-chair but did not get an immediate response. I was a little upset because I needed her to come *NOW*. I refused to wet my bed, even though I had a pad on the mattress. So I rang the buzzer again for my nurse, but by the time the nurse arrived, I had already used the potty and returned to my bed. And so that day ***I did it!*** I was a bit nervous, but I got out of my bed without assistance! I told the nurse what I had done and she was really proud of my accomplishment. She informed me, however, I needed to be extra careful and that she would be available if I needed her. I was so proud of myself and knew it was God who put the desire in me to trust Him, get up, and do it. The medical staff was proud of my progress and from that day forward, this particular nurse called me *Miss Independent*. That new name was music to my ears. I was not upset about her delayed response anymore. Jesus knows how to turn it around! That nurse's delay turned out to be the stimulus needed for my leap of faith. *"Delay is not denial"* became a reality for me. The nurse's delay that day worked in my favor. What a day of celebration for me!

I often wished I had a video recorder in my room. I wished I had a video camera in my room while at McLeod Medical Center as well. It seems I missed out on a lot because I maintained only a few scribbled notes about my progress while at both places. However, I would like to thank God for **Lauren Sharpe**, my former speech pathologist at the HealthSouth Rehabilitation Center, for all of her services rendered to me. Her charismatic personality is sure to win your heart. Lauren is young, beautiful, energetic, and has a heart to help others. We immediately found favor in each other and always prayed during my speech sessions. We prayed for ourselves and for others. We even prayed for her father, Larry Sharpe, who had been diagnosed with cancer. (Sadly, Larry passed away less than two years after my release from rehab.) Lauren, with her beautiful smile, loves the outdoors and enjoyed talking about the hunting trips she had shared with her dad. She loves her family and often expressed that love during our conversations. She was instrumental in providing writing supplies and encouraging me to make daily notes about anything I chose. I mainly used the journal daily to help improve my writing skills. However, I chose to record the names of all of my visitors and those who telephoned me while a patient at HealthSouth. The more I wrote, the clearer I would think. As my health improved, I started writing more details for my journal, including the first time I independently showered and dressed myself. Near the date of my release from rehab, Lauren even persuaded me to sing one of my recorded songs to her. It was uplifting to know that I recalled most of the lyrics, despite the earlier episode of bleeding on my brain. Lauren said, in her professional opinion, I had exceeded her expectations. She was my kind of therapist! After leaving rehab, I continued the daily journaling. These words to me from Lauren Sharpe are a keepsake:

> *"I hope that I not only helped you, but, remember, you changed my life and prepared my faith to be stronger as God knew what my life was about to face with my father. You inspired and strengthened me in more ways than you know! Love you."*

While organizing some papers that accumulated in my disarrayed bedroom, I was pleasantly surprised to have found the card that Lauren gave me the day I left HealthSouth:

> *Evelyn, words cannot begin to describe the way you have touched and changed my life! You are an angel sent to me, for both of us to learn, inspire, and help each other! Thank you for everything!! As far as your rehab progress…EXCEPTIONAL! You are so dedicated, determined, and diligent with all you face. You let God fight the battle and give Him the glory, which is so inspiring. You have made great progress and are just a miracle. Please keep in touch! Love you!*
> *Your sister in Christ,*
> **Lauren Sharpe**
> **Florence, South Carolina**

I enjoyed my stay at HealthSouth. Though my memory was a bit impaired while confined to rehab, I brought home some fond memories. The most humorous thing that happened to me at HealthSouth occurred when a nurse tried to insert a rectal suppository, but hurriedly misplaced it. I know there was no salacious intent but I immediately decried that she hit the wrong target. That nurse apologized over and over and OVER again. Another humorous occurrence took place after a shift change and I was introduced to my male nurse. I was smiling when he took my blood pressure, but then he messed up when he told me that *he* was coming back to wash me. I was really embarrassed when he returned and I told him that *only my face needed a wash.* Ultimately, he washed my chest, but I told him candidly and relentlessly, *"I'll take it from here!"* The nurse kindly relinquished everything to me. I struggled to complete the task at hand and by the time I finished using my sore, needle-marked arm, my water was cold. Mission accomplished! I triumphantly rang my buzzer for my male nurse to return to my room. Yes, they called me *"Miss Independent"* on that shift for real!

After viewing a picture my son had snapped at McLeod, showing my real hair disheveled, I concluded I must have worn a wig the day of the accident. I assumed the collision knocked the wig off my head and it was never recovered. My husband informed me later, *"I left that old thing on the floor of your SUV. You didn't need it anyhow."* Well, I don't remember which wig I chose to wear that day. I don't know which color or what length is missing from my collection. I only wanted to retrieve that wig to commemorate my head was left intact in that tragic accident.

One day I asked an occupational therapist to wash my hair. As she combed my hair, she noticed my hair was knotted and she could not get the comb through a specific area of my head. I told her that my head felt a little sore in that area. She then assumed I had stitches in my head and I told her I was never treated for a wound on the back of my head. She reported this to my attending physician at HealthSouth who requested that one of the therapists take a picture of the wound for my file. By this time the wound had a scab. I asked my HealthSouth physician what could have possibly caused the wound. He said it probably was the result of me lying flat on my back for so long. My husband and I talked about it later and concluded that if it were the result of me lying on my back then the wound should be the shape of a circle rather than a line. Personally, I believe the laceration to the back of my head was considered secondary since my breathing was initially sporadic and of utmost importance during my stay at the

Evelyn Murray Drayton

McLeod Medical Center. Yet I endured the pain and was grateful for life.

Being independent meant a lot to me and I gave each day my best shot. Several workers at HealthSouth occasionally called me by my new nickname, *"Miss Independent."* Patience was of utmost importance because I had to allow time for healing. To be honest, there were times I felt like being disobedient and cheating on my workouts and doing things my way, but I didn't. I appreciate the therapists who trained me to bathe and dress myself. They taught me the correct way to get in and out of bed. They even trained me to get in and out of a vehicle while wearing my back brace. I literally had to learn some basic routines all over again. Many days I went to the gym in pain, and with swollen feet, but still I got out of bed and was ready for the day. Each day I gained my independence. Miraculously, I progressed through my rehab and quickly recovered. God continued to show me favor in this place. I ministered to the workers and to my visitors during my two-week stay. I even gave a word of knowledge to a few people and they knew no one could have told me those things but God.

I thank God for all of my experiences at HealthSouth. Initially, I had erroneously anticipated maltreatment due to my ignorance about such a facility. Though it appeared mostly elderly people were on my hall, the workers at this facility made me feel special. They really did provide excellent care for me. Crossing paths with others at HealthSouth positively impacted my life and several have shared that their lives were changed for the better because we met.

Even before I was officially released from therapy in Florence, home health care providers were calling my husband to offer their services for my in-home care. Some inferred they were pessimistic about my short-term healing and recovery. Surprisingly, an individual asked if the doctor was sending me home or did I just want to come home. I believe that person inferred that the doctor saw death approaching and was sending me home to die! A number of providers had heard of my massive bodily injuries and made the assumption that I would not have adequate assistance at home. A few private-duty workers called me and were amazed at the news of my improved health. With God's help, my improved condition had surpassed the expectations of many in the healthcare industry. Although I had become acclimated to my hospital room, going home to convalesce was a treat!

Home Again, But Not Home Alone

Prayer travels without intervention of man-made transportation and I believed it was time for me to pray in faith and head home. Many thought I would not make it, but God's loving touch brought me home. *I am truly a miracle.* The prayers of the righteous really do avail much. Russell had already made the house wheelchair accessible, so I was excited to finally witness the car door swing open and to see what it was like to enter my house again. With all my broken body parts still intact, my husband reared back the wheelchair and pushed me into the house. Yippee! I was finally inside my house again!

Now my husband had to push me up another ramp to get me to the den. I stayed in the den until I realized Russell was unloading some things from the vehicle and doing some other things outside. I unlocked that wheelchair and tried to move myself through several rooms of the house. It was a struggle to roll that wheelchair over the soiled shag carpet that three rambunctious boys once roamed. Yet I was so grateful to be alive and able to wheel myself through parts of the house downstairs. When Russell came back into the house, I was huffing and puffing. He immediately said, *"Honey, you need to lie down and get some much-deserved rest."* Well, he did not push me into my bedroom to rest. *Guess which bedroom I had to stay in?* That's right—*the same bedroom I prepared before I left home on the day of the accident. I couldn't have known beforehand to prepare that bedroom for my*

Evelyn Murray Drayton

return from a hospital. Russell suggested that room because the waterbed in our bedroom was not firm enough for my broken body parts. When I entered the room, I looked at the bedding and said, *"Oh, Russell, it is so sweet of you to prepare this room for me. I like it."* Russell looked at me and said, *"What are you talking about? I haven't been in this room since your accident."* For some reason, I cannot remember this bedding and I don't have a clue how long it has been at my house. I am still trying to figure out when and from where I purchased the set.

I enjoyed being home again. My first morning at home was a blessing indeed. I took time just to think about my journey of tragedy to triumph. Like many other patients, I experienced fears, tears, worries, and hopes. I experienced setbacks, disappointments, and a flood of self-doubt. I even experienced laughter, anxiety and mood swings. In the Bible, the character Job experienced months of trouble. I knew my recovery had already exceeded a few months and I did not want to be an invalid for the rest of my life. My biggest fear was being confined to a wheelchair and having to rely on my husband. He was already committed to cooking my food, washing my clothes, assisting with my personal hygiene, etc. Whatever I needed, my husband was there. I was hoping he didn't get tired of hearing me call him so frequently for service. I did not want my husband to become my slave by caring for me both day and night. I also feared being a burden and not being able to perform my wifely obligations. *I believe that love is not a burden because we keep giving love away and love keeps replenishing itself.* And I can honestly say that my husband gave away a lot of love to help expedite my recovery. Yet I had to rebuke the fear that tried to overtake me. As you might imagine, I needed more than my bones to heal; I needed inner healing also. I didn't know if my memory would totally return. I did not know if I would be able to drive again and stay in my lane when meeting oncoming highway traffic. My kneeling prayer life suffered and my Bible reading was at a standstill. There were days I did not feel like praying, reading my Bible, or reading any other materials. I did not even want to watch television. Come to think of it, I don't recall having a Bible in my hospital room. One thing I did for sure was meditate on the word of God that I had hidden in my heart. I know the word of God is sure and stands forever. Intuitively, I was living on the prayers of others and kingdom deposits I had made earlier in life. And, of course, I remember Jesus Christ is our mediator!

In spite of all the major surgeries, I was able to slowly get out of bed, sit in my wheelchair, and roll myself to the bathroom to wash up. Although the house has two downstairs bathrooms with tub and shower combinations, I could not lift my legs to get into either of them. Unfortunately, my walk-in shower was upstairs and I could not walk up the stairs. I readily became acquainted with washing in the sink. I yearned for the day I could walk to the second floor of my house. I looked at my stairwell and told myself that *"I WILL walk those steps again."*

During my first full day at home, I continuously received telephone calls and visitations. I resumed journaling the names of my visitors just as I had done at HealthSouth rehab. My friend, Mary Canteen, brought my family a full-course dinner and spent the day with me. I spent most of my time on the couch, wearing my back brace and talking about my near-death experience and the goodness of God. I was glad that I made it through this day and I looked forward to the rising of the sun another day. As days went by I felt tired and a little lethargic. It seemed no matter what hour of the night Russell passed my room door, I was wide awake. *Why couldn't I sleep?* Starting with day four after my home arrival, my husband did not allow anything to disturb my rest. He demanded that I ignore phone calls, door bells, and knocks on the door. I did not realize the toll taken on my body, so his restriction was one of the best measures he could have placed on me. My tired and restless body recuperated nicely. With the calm atmosphere, the interchange of hot coffee and hot green tea was tasteful and relaxing. I drank more coffee and tea than I had ever in my entire life. One extra benefit to the hot drinks was using heat transfer from the hot cup. I would place the hot cup on my injured body parts and the result was immediate pain relief. I believe that my heat therapy translated into a faster healing and recovery.

My attention was drawn to our waterbed. I really wanted to lie on that waterbed! Maybe I wanted to lie on that bed so that I could throw my legs over Russell like I always did before the accident—I don't know. I got away with doing that during the winter, but he didn't like for me to throw my legs over him during the summer! *Well, it just so happened to be summer that I returned home from rehab.* In spite of my handicap, I still wanted to lie on that waterbed. Well, being the person that I am, I challenged myself to lie on that bed. I got out of my wheelchair and stretched out on that waterbed. Boy, it felt good to set that goal and reach it…for a little while. *The problem occurred when it was time to get off the bed.* Silly me! I planned how to get *on* the bed, but I did not plan how to get off. I could not wiggle like I needed to because of the back brace I failed to remove before I got on the bed. I could not bend my knees like I needed to because it was too painful. The only thing I could do now is call for help (in my hoarse voice): **"Russellllllll! Russellllllll! Please help me get off this waterbed!"** He came to my rescue—fussing all the way! When all the dust settled, he showed me the best way to get on and off the waterbed by myself, *in case I challenged myself again.* Then, sometime later, at my request he allowed me to lie on the waterbed beside him—only I had to promise not to throw my legs over him. Well, I was not physically able to *"throw my legs over him"* and he knew it. What a comedian!

Amedisys Home Health Services

Within days of being released from HealthSouth Rehabilitation in Florence, Amedisys Home Health Services of Georgetown provided my occupational and physical therapies at my house. I received about a month of in-home health care from three of their beautiful, caring therapists, **Janice M. Staten** of Georgetown, **Kristen Mattar** and **Drue Taylor**, both from Pawleys Island, South Carolina. The ladies, first of all, praised my recovery and ensured my accommodations at home were structurally sound with proper wheelchair access. They approved the temporary removable ramp my husband had built to get me in and out of the house. I did not like the ramp because, mentally, it seemed my wheelchair would overturn, even with my husband's assistance. Russell said he made a removable ramp because he did not anticipate me having to use it for long. My husband's few powerful words encouraged and motivated me! I refused to disappoint him.

The therapists taught me best practices for getting in and out of bed, maneuvering around the house, exercising my broken back, hip, and legs, and even how to independently maintain personal hygiene. They ensured I took my medication properly and kept check on my vital signs. After only six days at home, I was able to put light weight on the broken leg and I was so excited. ***By the way, they suggested that I not try to sleep in the waterbed! Again!***

Still on weight-bearing restrictions, therapy gave me the tools to deal with my recovery and confidence to move forward. I believe that anything is possible for I know with God, "*nothing is impossible.*" I superimposed my physical weakness and operated in God's strength. With in-home physical therapy and several doctors' visits later, my body continued to mend. There were times I wanted to massage my legs and feet with warm lotion, but that was only wishful thinking because doctors instructed me not to bend. I was so glad when I could bend and touch both my knees, calves, feet, and finally my toes. For a long time I could not experience maximum sensation to my body parts due to nerve and tissue damage. Nonetheless, my body continued to mend.

I was glad for each of the therapists' scheduled arrivals at my home so that we could share personal stories and hear their praise of my rehabilitation progress. At first I was reluctant to take my pain pills for an extended period, even with the doctor's blessing. I kept thinking how I lost one of my sisters to drugs, among other misfortunes. My doctors understood my overwhelming desire to remain a drug-free *church lady*. Yet they all encouraged me to take my prescribed medication, as needed, because they had my best interest at heart. Despite the initial reluctance, once the therapy sessions accelerated to stretching and exercising my broken leg, I gladly took my pain pills! (Kristen, Drue, and Janice—you smiled right there, didn't you?)

I had been bedfast for a number of days already, but the doctor gradually increased my weight-bearing status. The doctor vehemently urged daily walks, so I had to challenge myself to get up and practice walking. Many days I was up early and practicing how to walk before the school buses passed the house. I realized I could not make progress based on feelings and could not allow my weak feelings (physically or spiritually) to overtake me. After a few doctor visits, one of the therapists was informed of my increased weight-bearing status (still less than 100 percent) and she heightened my challenges to walk. As the doctor released me to put additional pressure on my left leg, I was able to gradually ease myself into the kitchen. One day the therapist instructed me to use the wheelchair and roll myself to the kitchen. Then she told me to get out of the chair and brace myself against the counter, standing gently on my once-broken left leg for the first time since the accident. This was my first day standing! It was painful, but I was so excited because it had been nearly four months since I had stood or walked on *two* legs.

Now that my body was stronger, I wanted to do more chores around the house. I know I had to be careful and not participate in any strenuous activities. I recall one day I took the helm of my wheelchair and rolled to a piece of dusty furniture. I took my finger and wiped dirt—not dust—from the furniture and asked my husband to wipe away the *pile of dirt*. My husband looked at me and said,

"That's the same pile of dirt you left on the furniture before your accident. Get well and you'll be able to clean all the dust soon!" Instantly, I had a moment of acute nostalgia about not having to do any work in the hospital. And here I was, trying to volunteer my *supervisory service* around the house and it was not appreciated. I debated whether I should laugh or get angry over his comment—well, I did both. I laughed because it was *partially* true. And I became angry because the truth hurts when you're guilty. I accepted his challenge to *get well so I could dust*! Russell's statement was embedded in my mind and motivated me to continue my exercise regimen as I repeated: *Get well, so that I can dust!* Ironically, I detest dusting, and Russell knows that well!

When the doctor, out of the blue, increased my weight-bearing to 100 percent, I was in a state of euphoria and rejoiced and celebrated as best I could over the good news. The doctor said it seemed I healed faster than normal! Releasing me from the weight-bearing restriction gave me the freedom to put full weight on both legs. So the first thing I aimed to do was get in the shower. With my mending body parts I could not step into the bathtubs or showers downstairs, neither could I climb steps to the walk-in shower upstairs. **What's a girl to do? I had to settle for the sink a little while longer!** I kept declaring that I would walk upstairs and I would get into my shower again. My husband continued to prepare delicious hot meals for me; the therapists continued to help me exercise; and God continued His healing.

After a short period of time, seemingly a *long*, hot summer, the therapists taught me how to maneuver my way up and down the staircase. My back and leg problems still restricted me from climbing into the downstairs bathtubs. **Guess what?** With my husband's support, I slowly climbed that stairway, one foot at a time, and headed straight to the walk-in shower upstairs. I made it—and I stayed in that shower a long, long, long time. I splashed water all over my head and back as if I were in a waterfall. I was another step closer to my independence.

The water felt so good running through my hair. Yet I continued to pay attention to the injury to the back of head, which was detected while at HealthSouth. Months after my hospital release, I saw a note in my McLeod's hospital records indicating *"healed laceration to back of scalp."* I stand to be corrected, but I don't know how it was healed while I was a patient there because it was still a sore after I was homebound. Maybe they thought my scalp was healed because my hair had matted and covered the wound. Even so, one day as I washed my hair at home, the entire horizontal strip of scalp and hair from the back of my head fell off. I took a picture and only then did I consider the wound totally healed.

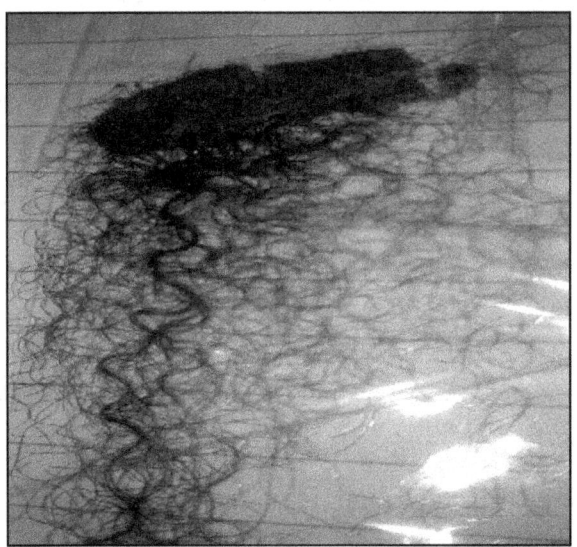

An object must have hit my skull—no wonder I was knocked senseless by the blow for a short period! Though I still have a bald spot with a dent on my head—I'm not crazy. So don't underestimate me and think there is a hole in my head when I forget things!

I had met another goal when I climbed upstairs because this fostered a lot of optimism. In addition, my standing and walking exercises continued with noticeable improvement. I laugh sometimes when I recall Janice elatedly announcing to me that I was able to independently stand at the sink and **wash dishes**. Upon my next scheduled session, she asked if I had already shared the good news with my family. I said, *"No, ma'am."* She disappointedly asked, *"Why not?"* I responded, *"I am not going to tell my husband and boys that I can wash dishes because they might also expect me to wash the pots and pans too."* We both laughed! When I felt mentally comfortable, I shocked the family by independently standing at the sink and making lots of noise banging the dishes—silverware, glasses, pots and pans—the whole shebang. I did not tell them the good news, I demonstrated the good news! That noise got their attention and we were all so excited! They wanted me to heal, but, surprisingly, **they didn't try to stop me from washing all those dishes!**

    I had to learn how to talk, write, and walk again. I had transitioned from wheelchair confinement to a walker and now to a cane. What an accomplishment for me! I most certainly enjoyed the interaction with my therapists and am appreciative for all they did to help in my recovery. Again, I thank you three ladies for not just doing a job—but also offering encouragement filled with love and kindness on each visit. God bless you always.

Nextstep Rehabilitation Services…and beyond

    Though the in-house therapy was beneficial and had accomplished its purpose, my primary physician wrote a prescription for additional extensive strengthening techniques. I registered at the local outpatient rehabilitation center, where a variety of equipment was readily available for physical therapy sessions. The therapists encouraged me to exercise my legs and to stop being afraid to put my full weight on my damaged leg. I chose to walk and endure pain that migrated from my damaged leg to my damaged hip, and also to my broken back. My legs and hip continued to strengthen as I continued my walking regimen. Many in the neighborhood saw me hobbling down the highway—limping on my cane. Passersby could not see the angelic forces encouraging me to limp a few more steps on my numb and swollen feet! I had to visualize my feet healed, so I purchased two pairs of oversized, inexpensive shoes to accommodate the swelling. It also occurred to me that rain or barometric pressure changes affected my pain level and my mental status. Many days as I limped in pain, it appeared the damaged leg had shrunk and was noticeably shorter than my right leg. I even asked my boys whether or not one of my legs was shorter than the other. Their responses were always, "*No, ma'am!*"

I continued to walk slowly, but with confidence. On one occasion, someone complimented my walking progress while my husband was present. My husband said, "*Yeah, I have her walking quite well now. When she acts like she doesn't want to walk, I just get behind her with an opened jar of wasps or bumblebees and she manages to pick up some speed. I'll have her running soon!*" My husband, Russell, is the comedian in my house!

Russell had driven me to all of my out-of-town appointments while I cautiously drove mentally and verbally from the passenger side. My behavior must have been frustrating for him. I had to rebuke the fear that tried to overtake me as I traveled the dangerous highways. A few people even said that I would be afraid to get behind a steering wheel again, and for a while I agreed with them. When the doctor said it was all right for me to drive, I set a goal to drive myself to outpatient therapy. One day it actually happened. My husband handed the keys to me—and I was behind the wheel proudly driving to my scheduled therapy session. Russell rode with me the first week and felt comfortable that I could handle things. To my amazement, I started driving my vehicle and would sometimes get out of the vehicle, leaving my cane on the seat. My gait was still a little bit off, but today my walking cane is gone and so is my limp. Ultimately, the numbness is dissipating and my severed nerves have regenerated enough that I can actually feel normal sensation in my feet. When I noticed I could manage without the cane, I assiduously pursued my goal of independence.

    One night I made several attempts to independently lift myself from the recliner—but to no avail. I then beckoned my husband to help me. He was watching a game on television and apparently did not notice that I had tried several times to release the lever on the chair. When I called him the second time, he looked at me affectionately and said, *"Go ahead and get up. You can do it."* When he told me that, I became irate because I had already tried several times. Immediately, out of frustration, I tried to leap from the chair while still in the reclined position and almost fell on the floor. My foolish action could have precipitated another crisis in my home. My husband came to my rescue, but he was livid because I was too impatient. He yelled, **"You see what you did? You could have paralyzed yourself!"** His tirade ended abruptly, but there appeared to be an escalation of conflict in my home that night. Russell was perturbed because he saw the danger I selfishly presented, not taking into account all the family had already endured. Jumping from that recliner was detrimental to my peace, so I wheeled myself to my bedroom and cried like a baby. I prayed, I repented, I thought about *what could have happened*. When Russell came to my room, I was still crying and magnanimously begged for his forgiveness. He waited a while and then apologized for his behavior as he hugged me. I knew he had forgiven me.

    This fiasco taught me that we have to forgive as well as accept forgiveness. Forgiveness releases the pain from both parties involved. I could not go to sleep that night without setting my house in order. We, as Christians, must be willing to forgive those who have wronged us. We cannot take matters into our own hands. Vengeance belongs to God. We may not want to believe it, but our anger, our frustration, and even our fears are under our control. For this reason, it is not a matter of "can we forgive." It is more so "Are we willing to forgive?" Will we make that choice to forgive? Isn't it amazing how we get over the hurts from our courting or dating days and can now laugh and talk with those same gals or guys who once hurt us to the very core of our hearts. So you see—we can forgive!

It would be wrong to ignore our frustration or anger, but we must make choices that deal with those feelings. We must take our thoughts captive as they surface so that they do not become strongholds. We must forgive! Forgiveness is not an option. *"God commands us to forgive."* Mark 11:25 lets us know that when we stand praying, we must forgive if we have anything against anyone. This reminds me how King Hezekiah had to set his house in order (2 Kings 20:1). Russell's love gave me the impetus I needed to move forward; and I knew better than to lock up my blessings and peace by not forgiving and setting my heart in order. Life is precious and death is always waiting at the corner. So don't allow cobwebs to be built in your heart—forgive!

> *"Teach and cheat have the same letters. If you don't allow Holy Spirit to TEACH you, you might try to CHEAT your way through life."* E. M. Drayton

Chapter Two

God Restores Health

"For I will restore health unto thee, and I will heal thee of thy wounds, saith the Lord...." (Jeremiah 30:17).

The most paramount question was whether or not I believed God could fully restore health and strength to my body. Not only did I rebound from a physical setback, but I also experienced an awesome mental and emotional recovery.

Evelyn after the accident, winter 2014

I knew in order for me to do what God had spoken in the past about my future, I had to believe; **YES**, I had to believe. Most assuredly, God is my healer and I believe the words spoken over my life **SHALL** be fulfilled. God is my healer and I can call Him Jehovah Rapha without reservation. I am no longer fearful of life or death and welcome each day with confidence. Jesus healed when He walked this earth, and He is the same Healer today as He was yesterday. Thank God for grace, mercy, and favor. Whatever I ask my Father in Jesus' name that lines up with His plan, He will do it. There comes a time when we can no longer look at our condition, we must remember our mission, our assignment on this earth, and know that we will live until it is fulfilled.

I had heard the word that Jesus is a healer, but believing that word by faith has been an awesome journey. Faith is *the substance* of the healing I hoped for (Hebrews 11:1). I know other people were praying for me and, according to Matthew 9:29, it was *my* faith that took me a long way in my recovery. In that Scripture Jesus states: *"...According to your faith be it unto to you"* (Matthew 9:29). No matter what the condition, I am to remember that He is the God that heals me. The horrific accident I experienced has totally changed my life. I believe I am much smarter now and tend to make wiser decisions. I remember thoughts of doubt and death, but I recall fighting in my mind with Scriptures that I had memorized. My mind continued to heal miraculously from the traumatic memory loss as I thought on God's word. I fought death every inch of the way. I believed that my Heavenly Father never left me alone and that He would help me recover from my injuries. I believed that my accident had a purpose and that things would work together for my good because I am called according to God's purpose. I am a very didactic person and really love teaching, so I was in the perfect setting to be an instrument in God's hand. If no one else knows of any good that came from my accident, I will raise my hand with an answer. ***I can witness to God's healing power and say how God ministered to others through me from my hospital bed.*** I had actually progressed faster than many had anticipated, including the doctors—**they said so**. Though I suffered substantially, I am at such peace and far more content than I could imagine, considering my struggles and challenges. I did not require any professional counseling because the Holy Spirit advised me every day. Scripture tells me to bless the Lord and forget not all His benefits (Psalm 103).

Though we are inept in the ways of God, the Word tells us to *"learn"* of Jesus and *"study"* to show ourselves approved. The more we study and learn, God will work through us to make us look like Him. When He is finished with us, we are better prepared to reflect His image through our daily living. We are still on this earth to reflect His image, to be a witness, and to be a testimony this side of Heaven. God is still working in our lives; and as a result, we can continue to live full and rewarding lives.

Retrospectively, on Wednesday, June 5, 2013, I was scheduled to be the guest speaker at Saint Paul African Methodist Episcopal Church in the Plantersville Section of Georgetown where the Reverend Rubin Smalls held the pastorate; my accident occurred on June 2. The news had circulated about my accident and an interim speaker for the Lay Organization of Saint Paul blessed the congregants with a soul-stirring sermon. I am honored and humbled to say that a last-minute decision was made to dedicate the June 5 services in my honor. Various churches in the community were invited and given an opportunity to share how I had impacted their lives. Several persons were mesmerized with sadness and offered many inspiring words of faith and hoped for my speedy recovery. I give special thanks to Reverend Smalls for allowing a copy of the DVD recording of that special service to be reserved for my viewing after my hospital release. That humane act reveals that someone had faith that I would live and not die.

I am told that the pastor made an appeal early on for visitation to be limited to family members only to give me time to recuperate. I am grateful, however, that Reverend Smalls, along with a few other church officers, visited me during my hospitalization and also at my home upon my return. I vaguely recall the faces of a few visitors, but very little of our conversations. My visitors probably thought I could feel their touch, hear, and even understand what they were saying to me, but many times I didn't. The long-term and short-term memory ordeal lingered for a while. I forgot many discussions in a matter of seconds. People would talk to me during the day, but I probably incorporated their daytime conversations into my dreams. My son, Justin, was instrumental in deciphering a conversation between Reverend Smalls and me. I know I probably talked a lot, but I only recall saying, *"Reverend Smalls, people need to hear the truth about Jesus. It's not about money and fame."* I cannot explain why I remember only that statement among all the other discussions we might have had. One Sunday after my return home, the pastor jokingly said from the pulpit, *"Dr. Drayton, some who visited you thought they were seeing you alive for the last time."* Seriously though, a few people said they had heard I was already dead and was just lying there until my husband gave the doctors approval to shut down the life-support equipment. Yet I am very appreciative for the people who adjusted their schedule and burned their gas to share a few minutes in my room.

The love and prayers of my family and friends, community and church members, and even some strangers helped me to miraculously recover from my life-threatening injuries. Reverend Smalls had been and still is exceptionally supportive in presenting ministry opportunities for me to share my spiritual gifts. The community, by and large, continues to express strong support for my well-being and ministry endeavors. Upon my release from the hospital and rehab, I became very emotional as I viewed the DVD from the June 5 church service and was honored that I was thought of and held in such high esteem in the community. I continued to be showered with love as I received visitations, cards, flowers, live plants—and, yes, some money. I recuperated speedily and overcame many adversities along the way. My healing case was not impossible!

Day 47—The Fulfilled Prophecy

Prophecy is a gift administered by the Holy Spirit and can provide teaching, correction, instruction, guidance, and direction that are supernaturally and divinely inspired to accomplish God's purpose. The gift of prophecy helps build up and edify or stirs believers to help fulfill our God-given assignments. Prophecies can help build up by helping to prepare and equip us for some future circumstances or events. Prophecies can help us avoid unforeseen circumstances and alter our course of action for future plans—all to help fulfill God's plan and to help us reach our destiny.

> *"And it shall come to pass in the last days, saith God, I will pour out of my Spirit upon all flesh: and your sons and your daughters shall prophesy, and your young men shall see visions, and your old men shall dream dreams"* (Acts 2:17).

God doesn't always use those of high notoriety to deliver His inspired messages. I can truthfully say that God has used famous people, as well as the unknown, to help offer direction, guidance, and instruction along the way to help me stay on course. Nonetheless, we must be careful because not everyone is sent of God or has matured in their prophetic calling. Allow me to clarify that prophecy is not fortunetelling. Fortunetelling, as far as I know, is the same as divination, which is satanically inspired. You do not need performance enhancement drugs for spiritual strength or hallucinogenic or psychedelic drugs to make you see and know spiritual things. You do not need Satan's power to influence your life. You do not need to seek a familiar spirit, a witch, or other medium to know about your future.

I have had false prophets speak things I knew were not God-inspired words. They were on assignment from Satan to cause havoc in my life. I have had people use numbers time after time in prophetic messages to me. Some time periods ranged from 24 hours up to 90 days. As a matter of fact, one false prophet, who is now deceased, told me years ago that he would bury me in 90 days if I told he was practicing witchcraft. (I said "false prophet" because I exposed him—and I am still alive.) So you should not totally rely on what man says is God-uttered word. You must seek God for confirmation to what He has already spoken to YOU.

I have been writing and recording my prophecies for a number of years now as they are shared with me. In earlier years, I really didn't understand the operation of the prophetic gift and the associated blessings. Therefore, I made a few notes here and there, but was never serious about confirmations. At one point it seemed not one prophetic word came to pass. Can I be honest right here? There was a time that I didn't want to hear another prophetic word from anyone. In the early 1990s, I started seriously seeking the Lord and recording many of the prophecies spoken over my life. I became so serious that I typed my prophecies, pasted them on my bedroom wall, taped a copy in my Bible, and even laminated a copy to carry in my pocketbook. I did not beg or persuade anyone to prophesy to me. As God's people spoke into my life, I activated my faith and moved forward on the uttered word. I can truthfully say that God has used His sons and daughters to help give me guidance and instruction along the way. The prophets were saying, "God said..." and I believed it. I am determined I will not let go of promises that belong to me.

God knew beforehand that on June 2, 2013, I would be involved in a near-fatal accident. Even though I had a horrific, near-death experience, God allowed the right people to be in place and on duty at the right time to help care for me. The accident, which I cannot remember, allowed me the opportunity to minister to many people who may forget me, but never the God who used me in the hospital to bless them and accomplish His purpose. Maybe I was on assignment like the biblical character Jonah! Who knows?

Weeks after being released from rehab and recuperating at home, I suddenly recalled that I had not opened my pocketbook since the day of the vehicle accident. As a matter of fact, *I had not even seen my pocketbook* since the day of the accident. I asked my husband if he had seen my bag—and he knew exactly where to find it. When he gave me the bag, I could hear glass rattling even before I opened the pocketbook. To my surprise, I found the napkin inside the bag that I had written the 47-day prophetic word given to me only hours prior to the accident. Despite the torrential downpour the day of the accident, miraculously not one word of ink on the napkin was smeared by the rain. I guess God really intended for me to read those words again!

It was exciting to read the words that I had recorded on the napkin. It is inferred that on June 2, 2013, I was minding my own business when the minister was led by God to talk with me. There was no prior discussion about any dates or numbers or anything else. As a matter of fact, we had not even spoken prior to this encounter. Furthermore, there was no one present at the time who knew that I would be in Florence that day. And there was no one in the sanctuary who knew me well enough to share any personal information with the prophet about me. Yet the prophet told me some things about myself as if he had known me for years. He unwaveringly mentioned some of my past hurt and pains. Just to recap from Chapter One:

> *Apostle Lance Jeter told me that I would witness a turnaround in ministry after **47** days. Amidst all*

> *his other prophetic words, the pastor was precise and adamant about the number 47. I was determined not to misconstrue the prophecy. I immediately retrieved and perused my notes, and thought to myself,* **"What can possibly happen in 47 days that would significantly impact the assignment on my life?"**

The minister prophesied that within 47 days there would be a turnaround in my ministry. He did not mention the word *accident* in the 47-day prophecy, but it is amazing how the 47 days panned out in my life. **Prophecy is real!** God allowed His message to reach my ears at such an opportune time. Undoubtedly, no other prophetic messages seemed to have significantly impacted my life like this 47-day prophecy. I don't fully recall my verbal response after Apostle Jeter released the prophetic words to me. I probably wanted to know why God told him 47 days—instead of 30 days, maybe. And, furthermore, I could have been tempted to ask him, "How did you know it was God who gave you those words to give me?" Knowing myself, however, I was probably teary-eyed and whispered to Apostle Jeter, *"Thank you for sharing those words with me."*

Miraculously, I arrived home in a wheelchair from Florence exactly **47** days after my accident. *Do you see that Number 47?* I may be an excessively scrupulous individual, but I don't call it a coincidence that the prophet hit the nail on the head with **"47 days."** Only God can strategize a message like that! I read the other words that I had written on the napkin along with the 47-day portion and got a fresher outlook on life. The number 47, independently, did not supersede the fact that God had me on His mind that day. I knew God was serious about His plan for my life and I had to partner with God's plan. As I read the prophecy repeatedly at home, I immediately started to set health recovery goals for myself. This prophecy had become a lifeline for me. For example, I set a goal when to stop using the bedside potty, when to stop taking my pain medication, and when to increase my exercise regimen. I was making sure I did not plan to fail. My life has never been the same since the prophecy and the accident. Though I faced an avalanche of health problems, my life was not over, it had only just begun! **I have truly witnessed a turnaround in ministry just as the 47-day prophecy revealed.**

While I do not proclaim to be a numerology expert, I knew there was something revelatory about the number 47 as the man of God ministered to me. Aside from the number 47, there are probably numerous people in the world who revolve their lives around numbers for various reasons. As a matter of fact, I was surprised to see the wealth of information on the web about the number 47. I recently found out there is even a club that invites people to share their stories about the number 47 and its relevance to their life events. Some people believe they have an innate sense of numbers and they believe that numbers have power. They may take into account that God from the beginning dealt with numbers.

It seems God used the numerals forty and seven quite frequently in Scriptures. In Genesis Chapter 7, for example, God expounded to Noah to take clean creatures on the ark in groups of seven. He told Noah that in the next seven days water will cover the face of the earth and the flood will last for 40 days and 40 nights. Genesis Chapter 8 shows a new beginning for Noah when the ark rested on Mount Ararat in the seventh month. The waters abated and Noah was able to open the ark's window at the end of the 40th day just as God had spoken to him about the rain. (There is that seven plus 40 = **47**, which was Noah's day of **victory**!). There is even a chapter in the Bible called Numbers. So, yes; I believe there is a spiritual purpose for numbers, even 47.

A greater revelation of the number 47 presented itself to me when Reverend Smalls asked me to be guest speaker for the Ash Wednesday service at Saint Paul AME Church. I was honored to be a spokesperson about God's word and, therefore, gladly accepted the invitation. I studied diligently for Ash Wednesday, February 18, 2015, knowing God had a purpose for allowing me to minister that night among all the other prolific speakers and other available dates. To my surprise, God gave me a crash course about my purpose for ministering at the Ash Wednesday service. The ministry assignment that night simplified and clarified how this speaking engagement date correlated to the number *47.* It was an eye opener for me indeed! Throughout the Bible, God gives messages that include numbers. For example, the numbers three, seven, and forty are used often in the Scriptures. So what was His message to Evelyn Murray Drayton about the number 47? There had to be a reason that I was chosen to be the speaker for February 18th. I had heard about the 40 days of Lent before, but I never thought twice about it. Inquisitively, I picked up a calendar and counted not 40, but 47 days, from Ash Wednesday to Easter, or Resurrection Sunday. There was that number 47! I don't know how accurate history is about the timing for all of Jesus' life events, but I am familiar with this annual celebration for Christians. The 47th day, to me, commemorates Jesus' victory! *I believe my 47-day prophecy spells victory for me as well.*

According to scripture, the Spirit, not Satan, led Jesus into the wilderness to be tempted by the devil. I thought about all the things Jesus had endured during His time on earth and how His close friends, the apostles, made decisions contrary to His teachings. They did not always show the brotherly love that Jesus had graciously taught them about laying down their lives for a friend. It doesn't sound like the disciples were all gathered around grieving while He hung on the cross either. Jesus hung on the cross; He suffered and died. The good news is Jesus arose; He got back up on Day 47 and is alive forevermore.

During my 47 days of health care in Florence, it seemed I was in a crucible of testing, but I was released on Day 47. I suffered deeply and nearly died a few times. *BUT* I had a Day 47! I know it is not a natural instinct to rejoice in suffering, but I am grateful for all God permitted. This prolonged medical situation brought about change in my life, but God had some favorable results in mind. God knows how to use adversity to advance us and make us look more like Him. He knows how to mold us and transform our lives. God let me know that my life will never be the same. He is rewarding me and restoration has already begun at my house—inside the building and inside my body. My crying days are behind me. No one can ever change anything about that completed chapter in my life. I am stronger and wiser than I have ever been. I have unspeakable joy and abundant love. God is rewarding me for maintaining my faith and enduring all for His glory. I know who I am, whose I am, and most importantly, I know The Great I AM. Now I am walking in victory! As Jesus rose with victory on day 47, so do I victoriously claim my day 47 as prophesied to me.

    My situation reminds me of Hezekiah who was at the point of death. He prayed and reminded God of his services. As a result, God added fifteen years to his lifespan. I don't know how many years I have left, but at least I did not die on the day of the accident. I thank God for the years I have already lived since the near-death experience. I bless the Lord for His mercy and for His favor and His wisdom.

    Just as there are maladies in our physical bodies, the enemy aims to bring about disunity in the church. Broken bones, dislocated joints, and torn muscles can wreak havoc in our physical bodies and also in the Body of Christ. It does not matter if the congregation is large or small. I noticed that there was not a broken bone in my knee joint; however, it seems I suffered the most discomfort in my left knee than from any of the other injuries. So sometimes it may seem like the church is healed because the people operate as though they are not broken. Yet underneath there could be hidden injuries that will bring about discredit and dishonor to God's people and inside the building we call church.

My physical injuries mirrored where the enemy was trying to attack me spiritually. He could not damage my eyes or my mouth. I can still "taste and see" the things God is showing me and I can still say those things He asks me to speak. As my body lay frail upon my bed, I know there were some things going amiss in the Body of Christ. Each of my broken parts represented an attack of the enemy in the spirit realm. Let's talk briefly about the partial anatomy of a saint (one who has accepted Jesus Christ as Lord and Savior).

> *"For as the body is one, and hath many members, and all the members of that one body, being many, are one body: so also is Christ"* (I Corinthians 12:12).

> *"For just as each of us has one body with many members, and these members do not all have the same function"* (Romans 12:4).

In my opinion, there are some important **"*impotent*"** people trying to lead God's people. These impotent leaders are like broken parts serving in the church with a need of deliverance or healing. Just about every part of the human body can be compared to a part of the Body of Christ because we are made in God's image. Knowing Christ is the spiritual head, the rest of the body can live. Christ is the head, so just where do you fit in? Are you a neck, an arm, a leg, or what? You are not the complete body all by yourself. **If Christ is not your head, then you are already dead.** A body cannot live without the head! You can be *important* (having power, high position, authority, and influence) but can still be *impotent* (lacking in power to act effectively; helpless to be used for an intended purpose). How can the blind lead the blind? Someone can be assigned to operate as a hand in the spiritual body. The main functions of a hand are to grasp, hold, and manipulate items—some may say the hand *gives to others*. Unfortunately, that same hand may want to function as a neck in the Body of Christ. The function of the neck is different than the function of the hand. Our human body can function without a hand, but the part will be missed greatly. However, the body cannot function without a neck. The main and obvious function of the neck is to hold up the head. The head and neck area is one of the most complicated anatomical areas in the body. God can decide to use an individual for any part He chooses. Nonetheless, the problem comes when God desires to use us for one part and we disobediently decide to serve as another part. Consequently, when God chooses someone to be a hand and that person operates elsewhere, the Body of Christ can experience malfunction and disorderly conduct, which can lead to ineffective and unproductive services. For that reason, let us reassess our situation and move to the point where God is operating and serve there. ***Victory!***

Areas I suffered during the 47 days

Our bodies are subject to injuries, since man is a spirit living in a body. From the physical, human, and natural standpoint, I should have died in my vehicle accident. I know God saw the intent of my heart and my will to live as His word states: *"Man looketh on the outward appearance, but the Lord looketh on the heart"* (I Samuel 16:7). The word also says, we *"shall know the truth"* (John 8:32). The truth in Exodus 15:26 tells me *"for I am the LORD that healeth thee."* So man is not my healer; God is my healer.

Many people prayed for me and I am eternally grateful for that kindness. I also made a withdrawal from my prayer account, knowing that God would heal me in Jesus' name. I had to believe that Jesus took my infirmities and bore my sickness according to Matthew 8:17. I believe in intervention of divine sovereignty and I saw God manifest His power in my life. My near-death experience reminds me of Hezekiah's experience and how God added fifteen more years to his life. God *"heard my prayers and seen my tears"*; but, unlike Hezekiah, God did not tell me how many years have been added to my life (Isaiah 38:4-5). Many days during my hospitalization, I had to do like David and *"encourage myself in the Lord"* (I Samuel 30:6). I had to believe that my prayer was an *"effectual fervent prayer"* (James 5:16). I had to believe that God will *"satisfy me with long life"* (Psalm 91:16). And always remember, *"He [God] sent his word, and healed them, and delivered them from their destructions"* (Psalm 107:20).

Analytically, each physically attacked area correlates to parts of our spiritual body makeup that needs to be on guard. Yes, I was torn, broken, and battered in all of these areas that are listed—all concurrently. The enemy wanted to wipe me off the earth. Have you noticed that you, too, have been spiritually attacked at some point in one of these areas as well?

Bleeding on the brain—Our thought patterns must be protected. God has given us a new mind, a new way of thinking. The enemy does not want us to think on the things of God—God's way and His thoughts. We are told to *"Let this mind be in you, which was also in Christ Jesus"* (Philippians 2:5).

Collapsed lungs and pneumonia—Holy Spirit is the air God's children breathe. It seems the enemy wanted to stifle me and shut up my intake of God's Spirit. Holy Spirit caused a spiritual transfusion that transported oxygen from the air into my bloodstream to remove carbon dioxide. This transfusion purified me from all intruders that might have invaded my surroundings while I tried to fit in to be one in the crowd. God took away those things that were not of His DNA.

Memory loss—If we are to believe that we cannot leave this earth until our spiritual assignment is completed then we need a change of mind. The enemy wants to strip us of God's words that are hidden in our heart and mind. Although there are things I do not recall, it is probably good for me that I was able to forget some secular things and move forward. God's word, my sword, reminds me that Apostle Paul, too, had to forget those things which were in his past. I cannot afford to allow memory of the wilderness to operate in my life. We as the body of Christ must continue to be obedient, knowing that we cannot remain in the wilderness when God has purpose for our lives. The enemy wants to blind our mind because we are changed by renewing our mind. God is restoring and bringing things to my memory; therefore, I cannot allow the voice of circumstance to override the voice of God. *"A double-minded man is unstable in all his ways"* (James 1:8). God keeps us in peace when we keep Him on our mind. What's on your mind?

Tracheotomy (ventilator)—My vocal cords were attacked and resulted in a raspy and hoarse sound for a few months, but my mouth was not totally damaged. The enemy has tried to silence my voice, but I have a brand-new voice. Therefore, the enemy cannot hinder me from talking about God and all He has done for me. I can still bless the Lord at all times by making a joyful noise unto the Lord and echoing praises from my mouth!

Broken left femur, kneecap damage, torn right femur muscles— These are the longest and strongest bones in my body (http://www.healthline.com/human-body-maps/femur). These muscles are near the center of my body. The muscles can represent the cords that are twisted together for strength and unity. *"A cord of three strands is not quickly torn apart"* (Ecclesiastes 4:12). God's children must realize we are ONE body. We need the support of our sisters and brothers in Christ. The enemy wants to attack those who pose the greatest threat to his kingdom. He wants to destroy those who can hold up some weight in the Body of Christ. The knee damage reminds me to kneel in prayer as the angels rejoice when I bow. He wants to close doors in my face, but I have a brand new walk. On Christ, the solid rock, I still stand! Doors *must* open unto me, one way or another. God says so!

Broken hip—It is amazing how the hip can help the body bear great weight. The enemy wants to dethrone us from sitting in heavenly places in Christ Jesus. Since Christ is seated at the right hand of God, and we are *in Christ*, then we, too, are sitting on a throne already hidden away in Christ. We, sons and daughters of God, *"sit in heavenly places"* (Ephesians 2:6). Can you picture that? Stretch your imagination!

Broken back—The back can carry the load for your body. Yet God has equipped us to bear the burden of our sisters and brothers in the church (Galatians 6:2). We must realize that we cannot even breathe correctly, depending which bone in our back is injured. When one in the Body of Christ hurts, another person also hurts! I know someone, somewhere, will be willing to help us should a need arises. Yet we must lean and depend on Christ because we have a firm support system in heaven. God has my back!

Fractured ribs—The ribs help protect other organs in the body. We must love and be willing to protect each other in the church. Interestingly, love was majestically manifested through Adam's rib in the form of a woman! We can't always explain why we cross paths with other people. Sometimes we are placed in the Body of Christ to surround and help protect others and they don't even realize why we are connected with them. They even try to get rid of us sometimes, but we may be *stuck* with them for a reason and only for a season. My husband and I met, but it was not our initial intention to get married. The same way I committed to giving myself to my husband only, I must also make a commitment to God and have no other gods before Him—none but HIM. God is my divine protection and He uses my husband to manage protection for our household. Now I understand how to have a more intimate relationship with my husband—and with God.

Lacerated liver—When the liver is damaged, the whole body seems to be out of synch. The liver helps to detoxify the body and the enemy does not want you or me to get rid of our old ways. The enemy wants to put us in bondage, so our old ways must be flushed away to prevent that. God's word cleanses, purifies, and washes us clean. *Have you had your spiritual flush?*

Stomach peg—The thought of a stomach peg sounds gross, but it serves as a necessary medical procedure for many patients, including me. If we are willing to eat spiritually, God can allow any means necessary for us to hear the word and get direction for our lives. God can even use social media, radio, telephone, smart phones, computers, dreams and visions, word of mouth from another sister or brother, or simply reading the word for ourselves. I must feed myself with the word of God. The peg reminds me of storage for the word—when I hunger, God feeds me. I want to eat food that is healthy for my spiritual growth. *Are you hungry—for the word of God?*

Nerve damage—Nerves are essential to everything that goes on in our body, yet they are fragile. Christians are the nerve center on this earth for accomplishing God's purpose, but we, too, are fragile. Some in the Body of Christ have become numb to the things of God. It no longer strikes a nerve to see and hear about disorder in the church. We often refer to sin as a sickness or a weakness. We no longer call sin a sin, which is defiance against God. My nerves were damaged, but the seasons have changed in my heart and in my life for the ways of God. Man can try to tamper with my life, but there are no locks that God cannot open. Despite my fragility, God's possibilities for my life are unlimited. I was already born in flesh and refreshed with health, but now my spirit is refreshed. What was done in me spiritually is now being manifested through me physically. My purpose will point me straight to my destiny. God knows how and when to open and close doors. He has given me new strategy and strength for my journey. My new anointing is not for me, but for the place God has sent me. I am who God says I am and have embraced my new place. I believe that I am a strong person and have a great future in life. God is allowing me to enjoy some of the finer things of life. I see His word, His plan, His promises, and His truths manifested in my life. I am fragile, but I am a miracle!

Life support—There are things that God allows us to do for ourselves. Yet we cannot make one of our organs function by our own hands. If you are to live in this world as a Christian, a believer of Jesus Christ, then you must be kept alive by the word of God. The word is your life support. God sent His Holy Spirit to live in us to seal us until the day of redemption. Our lives are hid in Christ. God has a way to sustain us when it seems all hope is lost. When we are weak, God is still strong. I was sold out to sin and Jesus Christ gave me new life. The old Evelyn died and I am now walking in newness of life—and this life is more abundant.

I do not know all of the people who visited me when I was on life support. I did not find out until a year later (Friday, June 20, 2014) that one of my friends shared how she called the hospital and requested the nurse put the telephone to my ear while she prayed and read scriptures to me when I was in the coma. I am grateful to have such a sister of faith in Christ! According to Mark 5:34: *"And he [Jesus] said unto her, Daughter, thy faith hath made thee whole; go in peace, and be whole of thy plague."* Jesus told the woman, "thy faith"; so remember to pray and activate your faith. Make certain you pray while you have health and strength—don't wait until tragedy strikes. I felt in my spirit that some people were upset when I mentioned anything about **my faith** being involved with my healing. Yet I am so blessed and so grateful that so many people prayed for me. I know people prayed for me! I know I prayed for myself prior to my accident also! But I believe and I know **GOD** is my healer.

Wherever problems exist in our lives, God has the remedy! A number of small items were vital during my recuperation: beds, chairs, medication, a breathing apparatus, bandages, ice bags, heat pads, a back brace, a wheelchair, a walker, a cane, exercise, a warm shower, food, water, love and support, laughter, smiles, tears, and lots of rest, to name a few among many. So I only listed a few items to remind you that *all* of those items listed were vital at different levels of my recovery. I intentionally omitted from the list wisdom, understanding, knowledge, skills—all of those God-given gifts. I did it to make a point—God will use whomever He wills and at whatever time He chooses. And, likewise, God has a plan for each of us according to His purpose. Although a chair was required, I did not use one while I was comatose, but I needed a chair later. Likewise, you may not be needed all of the time, but you need to be available for God's use at all times. He has prepared you and equipped you for His purpose and His plan. You never know when a situation arises that He needs you. Whatever you are experiencing right now, whatever your status, God has just the right place and time to use you so that you would be the most effective for His purpose.

> *"I can do all things through Christ which strengtheneth me"* (Philippians 4:13).

> *"When thou passest through the waters, I will be with thee; and through the rivers, they shall not overflow thee: when thou walkest through the fire, thou shalt not be burned; neither shall the flame kindle upon thee"* (Isaiah 43:2).

Even though severely injured, I was at peace in the hospital most of the time. Yet the enemy wanted to commandeer my life because he cringes when God's children are at peace. Peace is spiritual warfare and I believe Satan decided to setup temporary camp in my room to taunt me. Satan whispered, *"If God loves you, then why did He allow this to happen to you?"* Then I thought *"Why not me?"* I counterattacked in my spirit as I turned my eyes toward Heaven and said to my Heavenly Father, *"Be glorified through me, my God."* Don't allow Satan to lay a guilt trip on you or allow him to make accusation to you against your Heavenly Father.

> *"And as Jesus passed by, he saw a man which was blind from his birth. And his disciples asked him, saying, Master, who did sin, this man, or his parents, that he was born blind? Jesus answered, Neither hath this man sinned, nor his parents: but that the works of God should be made manifest in him"* (John 9:1-3).

While I lay in the trauma unit, I saw the face of a woman who I believed disliked me even before my accident occurred. I had a vision where the lady sat at the nurse's station to observe me from a distance. I recognized her face and it seemed my earlier inclination was solidified as God was confirming what He had shown me earlier. I kept waving my hand to get the lady's attention. She just stared at me, but never waved back, as if to taunt me. She displayed such atrocious behavior toward me, despite my medical condition! Now I know for sure that this lady is not my friend and that I need to be careful with her once I am released from the hospital. To ensure I was not hallucinating, I shared the details with someone at the hospital. Furthermore, while I was in consultation with hospital staff, that same lady's evil spirit entered my room and, all of a sudden, I just threw up for no reason at all. A staff member asked me why I didn't inform someone that I was nauseated and they could have had a pan at my bedside. I had the fortitude to share that I was not nauseated, but I was attacked by an evil spirit. The vomiting episode is even documented in my medical records. I shared that experience with only one person other than the staff member. Afterward, I asked one of my visitors to close the drapes to the door entrance because I did not want anyone *peeping* in my room. It was uncanny how I continued to feel the lady's presence lurk around to keep tabs on my medical progress. I found out everyone who smiles in your face is not your friend. I found out everyone who says they are praying for you are really not. I found out that just because someone gives you a gift doesn't necessarily mean it is given with the right motive. After praying, I later felt the presence dissipate. I saw *in the spirit* when a hospital security guard escorted the lady away from peering into my room and told her to not visit my room anymore—and, as a matter of fact, the security guard then banned her from entering the hospital premises. That security guard must have been an *angel*. I never vomited again that I am aware of during my entire stay. There are probably many others who dislike me, but I saw this one specific person. Why this lady is so jealous of me I don't know for sure. I wish I knew what specific trait fosters the enemy's jealousy so that I can praise God for that blessing even more. That lady probably doesn't know that I know her true identity—but I still pray for her deliverance. The enemy didn't give my blessings to me and jealousy won't take them away—I refuse to *give* them away.

It remains controversial whether or not Satan has to obtain divine permission to attack those of us who have accepted Jesus Christ as Savior. I believe it is true based on cases with biblical characters, Job (Old Testament - Job 1:9-12) and Peter (New Testament - Luke 22:31-32). Oh, and let us not forget how Satan attacked Jesus who arose and reigns in victory. I believe Satan had already attacked my character, my property, my children, and now he was permitted to attack my health. *(There are different beliefs about the "permission" teaching.)*

Though I was victorious with the first attack, evidently Satan was angry and unleashed demons in my room. When I locked eyes with those imps, they glared back defiantly. Satan's attacks are to subjugate God's children and to instill fear; in my case, fear of death. Apparently, Satan's objective was to instigate a little rebellion in me against God, but I was able to seize a divine moment. I refused to cower so that Satan could not steal my life. I know that I am a threat to Satan's kingdom because I know who I am. I know that God has called me to greatness.

I have never served in any branch of the United States military. However, we who accept Jesus Christ, along with angels, are God's military agents on earth. We must be trained and equipped the same way other military forces are trained. We must be introduced to weapons and learn how to use them effectively. The enemy studies his target, but does not fight fairly. We must, likewise, study the enemy, be vigilant, and always guard our hearts. Every effort should be made by God's children to preclude such ominous satanic attacks. I believe I actually fought demonic forces—or maybe I should say angels were fighting for and with me that night. It seems I felt angelic presence and heard the sound of wind from their wings fighting for me. I even recall seeing a white feather on my bed one morning, and I have no other explanation where that feather came from other than an angel being in my room. I believe that angel was real; I just don't know what happened to that feather. For an unknown reason, I had not shared my testimony about the feather being on my hospital bed. However, a prophetic word was given to me in August 2014, over a year later, detailing how angels were dispatched on my behalf and that God's angels did not even lose a feather. So, after listening to the minister, I now believe that the angel did not lose a feather, but gently placed a feather on my bed to encourage me and remind me that God had angels encamped about me as promised in Psalm 91:11. Courage was exemplified during the battles on my bed.

Furthermore, I believe God's angels fought death angels for my healing and they will continue to fight for me until God calls me home. I know angels were in my room! I had inside help (*Holy Spirit*) and outside support (*God's angels*) that God provides for His children. **NOTE: I believe angels are created beings that protect us from external opponents. Holy Spirit helps to prepare us internally to respond to external forces.** All during the day I could hardly wait until night for the angels to make their appearance again.

God is able to use us no matter our current condition. Even in a frail body, a person can still talk about the goodness of God. I probably escaped post-traumatic stress disorder that many others experience simply because I don't have any intrusive thoughts about the accident. However, during my recovery process, I constantly and consistently made adjustments in my life and I am becoming a trained and fully-equipped soldier in the army of the Lord. I had to change my state of mind and receive my promotion from God. I am a soldier among God's soldiers. I am taking one day at a time as I await instructions and guidance through the leading of God's Holy Spirit. As my restoration progressed, I learned that an unskilled speaker can still be knowledgeable of Jesus Christ. (I'm thinking about how the Corinthians poorly evaluated Apostle Paul.) As a matter of fact, one of my friends calls me one of God's generals. Even before the implied title of general, I dreamt that I had changed from my camouflaged combat fatigues and dressed in my service garb and boarded an airplane. I believe I am smarter now than before the accident.

I heard some amazing stories of God's healing power and divine intervention in the lives of many people. It seems many were anxious to share their stories as a means of encouragement for me to stand strong and remain focused for my healing. Though I suffered many internal and external injuries, I was able to look upon other people as examples of God's faithfulness to heal. I habitually celebrated my new opportunity at life and I was glad to see and chat with all of my visiting friends. They brought me puzzle books that kept me occupied and relaxed at the same time. I enjoyed being challenged and was able to focus on one thing at a time.

I had driven to town one day and while I was gone, a couple stopped by my house to visit and drop off some reading materials for me. My son did not remember the couple's names. To my surprise, all of the books were about *healing*! The couple never called or came back to visit. To this day, I still do not know who these people are. So, if you are reading this book and you are the couple, please contact me pronto. I would love to meet you. God is so good and I wouldn't be awfully surprised if the couple were angels who were dispatched to drop off these books to my house. I believe in angels and that's exactly what I had been thinking all of these years.

Through all of the excitement of having visitors, I still had to pay close attention to words that others spoke over my life. *"Death and life are in the power of our tongue"* (Proverbs 18:21). The word of God is power and His words must glide over our tongue. If words did not line up with my healing goals or what I believed, I immediately cancelled those words. For example, someone said, *"You might be walking without a cane in about a year from now."* I cancelled those words and I walked independently without a cane within only a few months. Someone else said, *"You will have to put up with your coughing and the hoarse voice because those symptoms normally don't go away when you have a trach tube installed."* I cancelled those words and my voice was back to normal within weeks after leaving rehab. A few people looked at me as if I were crazy a few times when I said, *"I renounce and cancel your negative words over me in Jesus' name."* I tried not to entertain any negative words because I had enough trauma, excitement, and negativity going on already.

In less than three weeks after returning home from the hospital, a few people started hating on me—just a few. Someone blatantly lied and said that I didn't want any visitors at my house. It was extremely heartbreaking to know the person who spread that egregious lie and to know the motive behind it. The Holy Spirit informed me that some people were jealous and upset because I recovered so speedily. I also found out that several people who told me they prayed for my recovery were really disappointed that I survived. I shared that revelation with one of my prayer partners and asked her to please keep my name in prayer. As a matter of fact, within a few days, the same message was proclaimed by a prophetic minister who publicly ministered to me in a local church and said: *"Dr. Drayton, your survival disappointed some people."*

My heart was broken when I **overheard** comments made by a few people I respected. One person angrily said, *"It ain't nothing she did why she's still living."* Another person said, *"She didn't have anything to do with her healing."* The same person also said, *"If she was living so holy, God would have taken her on home to glory."* An additional statement came from a well-known voice that I once held in deference more than I do now, even though I have forgiven. The person said: *"She ain't the only one who survived an accident. God let her live so she can get her life right."* It seemed as if they wanted me to feel guilty or to repent from whatever I allowed in my life that led to the vehicle accident. (Remember Job's three friends?) Now here is the bombshell statement: *"Why are they talking about her healing so much? There are other people in the community recovering from sicknesses too!"* It seemed a few haters devised a ploy and enjoyed the opportunity to tell me, *"You are not the only one who endured a little trauma."* You see, I can attest to God's healing power and how blessed I am to have recovered from my near-fatal injuries. At one point, it seemed one or two people were boisterously comparing and competing against my testimony to prove their heartbreaking stories of pain were more graphic or worse than mine. One person indicated **never** being involved in a vehicle accident, which goes to show that that blessing exceeded mine. In reality, God is glorified in each situation because we are both blessed and should be thankful for His diverse blessings.

Many are eyewitnesses to God's miraculous work through my life and you would think everyone would be happy that I am doing well! Unfortunately, I am aware of that one who is upset that I was given the opportunity to minister in a greater capacity after the accident. Why be upset by this? There is enough work in ministry for everyone to share in one way or another. Also, everyone has a testimony about something and will eventually have a platform to share it, if they are willing to do so. I don't understand all the jealousy and hatred. Conversely, the very act that the enemy planned to destroy me actually gave me a spiritual boost. This reminds me of the time when Jesus gave life back to Lazarus. People plotted to take Lazarus' life *again*. We cannot allow the enemy to make us relate suffering only to ungodly people and make inflammatory remarks against our sisters and brothers instead of speaking blessings.

I am honored to share the words of Brent Barnett who exhibits such strong teaching ability to help equip the Body of Christ:

> *There is a serious misconception that is becoming increasingly widely held within evangelical circles which teaches that, as believers, we have the right on this earth to have freedom from sickness, financial struggle, and, in fact, struggle and suffering of almost any kind and any nature. This position and line of thinking is so contrary to the full counsel of Scripture. Therefore, let us not suppose that suffering in this life is merely something due to a Christian lacking faith, but let us come to understand and believe that God has a plan and purpose in ordaining suffering for us in this life....We ought not to be surprised at difficulties and suffering in our lives. When it happens, we can be sure that God knows what is going on, that He is sovereign over our circumstances, and that He will cause all things to work for our good* (Romans 8:28). **Suffering is not a sign of weakness; rather, it helps us to see our weakness** [bold emphasis mine]. *It is only when we come to see, believe, accept, and embrace that we are helpless and weak apart from Christ that Christ can truly fill us, use us, and make us strong in His name for His kingdom purposes. It is suffering that produces character, endurance, and hope. Trials are not evil,*

pain is not necessarily bad, and suffering can be for our good.
#84 The Refiner's Fire: Sanctification Through Suffering
http://www.relevantbibleteaching.com by
Brent Barnett

    I thank Brent Barnett for expounding on suffering and I find the teaching beneficial. Generally speaking, there is a lack of teaching in many churches today. As a matter of fact, there is even a shortage of laborers to pray as well. Arguably, just because we are inundated with religious activities, not every religious person or churchgoer is a person of prayer. Yet I thank God there are still a few people available who pray earnestly and incessantly. We must be prepared for the waking and shaking of events in life and know how to be a people of study and prayer. We can know *who* and *Whose* we are by reading God's word. Some people may not even believe that God's word is true. That's our choice! Our *not believing* does not change who God is nor does it alter what God says. Many of us are so busy we don't know whether we have met or surpassed our goals of studying God's word. I am not surprised that many have even decided to stop setting goals. Why do I say that? Some people become discouraged when they face challenges in life and somehow feel they have failed God. In actuality, they did not fail God, but possibly misapplied the word.

    The Lord allowed me to enjoy life even in the midst of tragedy. Our Drayton family reunion is held every two years and 2013 was the year for this planned event. It was a blessing to see faces of family and friends that I had not seen for a while. The food was delicious too, I might add. I thank God I was still alive to see the sunshine, realizing I could have been in my grave. In addition, on Sunday morning, October 20, 2013, the choir sang a song that set the church on fire: *"I am a living testimony. I could've been dead and gone, but Lord you let me live on."* How did I respond to that song? *Yes*, I walked up and down the aisle in tears of joy—even with my limp. *"Put thou my tears into thy bottle: are they not in thy book?"* (Psalm 56:8). Until God tells me to *sleep*, I *"shall not die but live"* to share the goodness of God and to manifest His glory! Another event took place this year that was dear to my heart. I was honored to represent the Plantersville Community as the Christmas parade grand marshal for 2013. I was blessed to offer lots of waves and kisses to my community as I rode in my cousin's luxurious Lexus Coupe. I also received various community awards. In addition, I landed opportunities to preach, teach, and share my testimony. Not only did I survive, but I am on my way to full recovery as I simply brag about Jesus Christ. I joyfully celebrate life as God presents opportunities to share.

  My husband and I celebrated 25 years of marriage while I was recuperating. My body was bruised and broken, but I was glad to be alive to kiss my husband's hand. Years ago when I planned my wedding, I had to stay true to who I am. I did not have a traditional wedding reception. I don't know what people did after I exited the facility, but I restricted alcoholic beverages and I played gospel music. I found out that I did not have to fit in and follow other people's agenda because God had already set me aside for His use. My decision may not have been popular, but I was happy with myself when the day ended. Still, to this day, I am proud of my boldness to be different. As a matter of fact, I continue to make unpopular decisions. I retired early from my job just when my salary had increased and things were looking pretty good. In addition, I have made unpopular decisions in the religious arena that hindered me from promotions, which I felt would have led to compromising myself and my morals. In the same way, some may have expected me to act differently after my miraculous medical recovery, but I am bold enough to remain true to who I am and not be manipulated by people.

Anything's Possible: The 47-Day Prophecy

My final doctor's appointment resulting from the accident was intentionally scheduled at my request for June 2, 2014, commemorating one year since the 2013 accident. The receptionist presented to me several dates to choose from but I was BOLD and requested June 2 to bring closure to that trauma chapter in my life. I wanted to build my confidence and prepare my mind to put the past behind me. In only one year to the date, I was medically released to pursue my life's dreams. Within one year, I had gained 11 pounds and was back to my preaccident weight. I had been released from the hospital, completed in-home and outpatient rehab, started driving again, conducted church seminars, gave radio and television interviews, accepted speaking engagements and attended various church events—the whole gamut—within this one year of recuperation.

I visited a church one night where prayer and healing services were held. To my surprise, I sat near the front and saw a young man confined to a wheelchair. My eyes stayed glued on the young man as inquisitiveness overtook me. I found an opportunity to converse with him and asked him about his wheelchair confinement. He told me that he was involved in a car accident about five years earlier. This young man had so many ailments, which included the need for an ileostomy bag at his side. When I looked into his eyes, I was reminded that my vehicle was totaled and that I could have been in the same condition as he. My outcome in life could have been so different than it is—it could have even resulted in my death. I prayed for the young man to recover, realizing both of us could have been dead. My traumatic and frightening accident caused a turning point in my life. I know it is a miracle that I survived and recovered from the horrendous crash. I looked at the young man again before we departed the church and thanked God for His amazing grace.

Nobody Knows the Trouble I've Seen is more than a song title to me. Seriously, no one knows my deep hurt or pain, only what I have chosen to share. My book, **Beyond Our**

Scars, was written years before my accident, but it included therapeutic materials for my recovery. I had a will to live. Though I am still mending, I have enough mobility and strength to return to my active lifestyle. I have made a remarkable recovery. Not only did I survive, now I can thrive. There are things I want to accomplish with my life. I thought about the word BEYOND and I knew without a doubt that I could move on the other side of my hurt and pain. I had to move FORWARD—move BEYOND the scars!

We really don't know how close to death we are at times. Holy Spirit informed me that I was closer to death during the witchcraft attack I suffered back in 2002 than I was from this vehicle accident. (Read my book: ***I Had to Die Exposing Witchcraft in the Church.***) You see, people across the United States prayed for me during my vehicular-crash episode. Contrarily, there were "friends" who would not even speak to me during the near-fatal attack I suffered from the hands of a warlock who was also a *man of the cloth*. It seems many church members were desensitized! It appeared no one believed my story while I agonized in isolation. It was absolutely grueling to find someone to share my struggle. The conclusion of the matter is this: if both friends and foes decried and refused to speak to me, I knew no one was praying for my deliverance during that period.

Yes, I know how to suffer. I have experienced life-threatening injuries and other catastrophic events in life. But, because I belong to God, I trust Him to cover me in every situation that He allows in my life. I don't know my limit; I don't know how much I can bear—but God knows. When we are confronted with problems beyond our control, we have a choice to change our perception of the problem. I have seen God use what I labeled a problem to help me become a catalyst and a conduit for His purpose and His glory. I want people to believe that God is a healer, but not simply because I am telling my story. I want people to hear God's Word and believe God's Word. I am only evidence or a witness that God's word is true. Jesus died for us and sacrificed Himself for all of our sufferings. When we hear God's word, we hear His voice. When we hear His voice, we must obey. It seems just as you choose to believe, Satan will challenge your decision and contest your fight of faith. Satan specializes in bringing doubt and discouragement. We must not let unbelief hinder our blessings. I read in the Bible that *unbelief* (Matthew 13:58 and also Mark 6:5) became an obstacle in Jesus' ministry: *"And he [Jesus] could there do no mighty work...."* When we serve God, it's not all about the telling; it's also about believing and showing. There comes a time we have to *show and tell*.

God has used my situation to show others His healing power. How can we assure others of healing if no one has ever been sick? God's healing power has been manifested through my life. Healing is still a gift to God's family. I believe the words that say: *"And these signs shall follow them that believe; In my name shall they cast out devils; they shall speak with new tongues; they shall take up serpents; and if they drink any deadly thing, it shall not hurt them; they shall lay hands on the sick; and they shall recover"* (Mark 16:17-18). Gifts of healing may not be my dominant gift, but I believe I am anointed to lay hands on God's chosen people and they shall recover according to His word. There is no failure in God; we then have to acknowledge that we are not using the power and authority that God has given us. There are some biblical stories of healing (II Kings 5:1-14; Acts 5:15; and Acts 19:12).

> *And Hezekiah said unto Isaiah, What shall be the sign that the* LORD *will heal me, and that I shall go up into the house of the* LORD *the third day? And Isaiah said, This sign shalt thou have of the* LORD, *that the* LORD *will do the thing that he hath spoken: shall the shadow go forward ten degrees, or go back ten degrees? And Hezekiah*

answered, It is a light thing for the shadow to go down ten degrees: nay, but let the shadow return backward ten degrees.[1] And Isaiah the prophet cried unto the LORD: *and he brought the shadow ten degrees backward, by which it had gone down in the dial of Ahaz* (II Kings 20:8-11).

Now Naaman, captain of the host of the king of Syria, was a great man with his master, and honourable, because by him the LORD *had given deliverance unto Syria: he was also a mighty man in valour, but he was a leper. And the Syrians had gone out by companies, and had brought away captive out of the land of Israel a little maid; and she waited on Naaman's wife. And she said unto her mistress, Would God my lord were with the prophet that is in Samaria! for he would recover him of his leprosy. And one went in, and told his lord, saying, Thus and thus said the maid that is of the land of Israel. And the king of Syria said, Go to, go, and I will send a letter unto the king of Israel. And he departed, and took with him ten talents of silver, and six thousand pieces of gold, and ten changes of raiment. And he brought the letter to the king of Israel, saying, Now when this letter is come unto thee, behold, I have therewith sent Naaman my servant to thee, that thou mayest recover him of his leprosy. And it came to pass, when the king of Israel had read the letter, that he rent his clothes, and said, Am I God, to kill and to make alive, that this man doth send unto me to recover a man of his leprosy? Wherefore consider, I pray you, and see how he seeketh a quarrel against me. And it was so, when Elisha the man of God had heard that the king of Israel had rent his clothes, that he sent to the king, saying, Wherefore hast thou rent thy clothes? let him come now to me, and he shall know that there is a prophet in Israel. So Naaman came with his horses and with his chariot, and stood at the door of the house of Elisha. And Elisha sent a messenger unto him, saying, Go and wash in Jordan seven times, and thy flesh shall come again to thee, and thou shalt be clean.[1] But Naaman was wroth, and went away, and said, Behold, I thought, He will surely come out to me, and stand, and call on the name of the* LORD *his God, and strike his hand over the place, and recover the leper.[1] Are not Abana and Pharpar, rivers of Damascus, better than all the waters of Israel? May I not wash in them, and be clean? So he turned and went away in a rage. And his servants came near, and spake unto him, and said, My father, if the prophet had bid thee do some great thing, wouldest thou not have done it? how much rather then, when he saith to thee, Wash, and be clean? Then went he down, and dipped himself seven times in Jordan, according to the saying of the man of God: and his flesh came again like unto the flesh of a little child, and he was clean* (II Kings 5:1-14).

Insomuch that they brought forth the sick into the streets, and laid them on beds and couches, that at the least the shadow of Peter passing by might overshadow some of them (Acts 5:15).

So that from his body were brought unto the sick handkerchiefs or aprons, and the diseases departed from them, and the evil spirits went out of them (Acts 19:12).

A friend told me the church is full of the *needy* and the *greedy*. For some reason, I thought she said, *nitty-gritty*. This is a conundrum to unchurched people, maybe, but there is some truth and clarity in both groups of words which probably can take up a whole chapter of explanations. Many leaders are avaricious if they serve in the church only for financial gain. Personally, I can say I owe my life for all God has done for me. I was indeed *needy* and became *greedy* for his presence. (I know that was not my friend's intended context.) It is impossible to pay God back for all He has done for me. He has taught me about *hope, faith,* and *charity.* I am grateful and honored to tell of His goodness as I write about my vehicle accident, which I don't even remember happening. I only know details that were shared with me through written reports and word of mouth. Just as God hid my sins in the sea (Micah 7:19), it seems He also hid the details of my tragic accident. I experienced healing from emotional, spiritual, physical, and relational episodes, all stemmed from one event. The accident occurred SUDDENLY and without warning, leaving me in a state that I had never experienced before. The prophet had warned me that Satan was trying to steal from me—I just didn't know it was my very life. I had never planned for trauma at all—the pain, the change, the stress, the uncertainty. My most recent book, titled **And Suddenly**, was beneficial to me. Little did I know how God would use my own books—just the titles—to bless my own life. Just as the accident occurred suddenly, so did my healing! I am a living witness of the faithfulness of God and I believe the best is yet to come SUDDENLY! I had to overcome the idea of *wishing* for a healing. I learned that I had to do more than hope; I had to believe. I am learning each day to sharpen my faith by believing, not just hoping. Faith pleases and moves God. I am learning to maximize my life by operating in faith.

Within four months of my accident, despite my myriad internal and external injuries, I gave a presentation, titled *Church Etiquette*, at the Saint Paul African Methodist Episcopal Church in Plantersville. During the presentation, I lifted the cross from the altar table to explain the purpose of its three steps (faith, hope, and love), not realizing the weight of the cross was too heavy for me to bear. My body was still weak, and I believe the audience could see I nearly dropped it. My friend, and a dedicated member of Saint

Paul, the late **Russell Anthony Bromell**, walked up to me and offered to bear the cross for me. Before I could ask for any help, he had detected the struggle and came to my rescue. I was grateful for Mr. Bromell's support and was glad I did not have to *bear that burden alone*. I was immediately reminded how Jesus carried His cross, but he was relieved of the weight and burden by a bystander who was compelled to carry the cross. The audience never knew how God ministered to my heart right in front of them while I succinctly concluded with tips for proper church etiquette. I longed to alter my presentation and discuss the eye-opening incident, but was limited due to time constraints. I wanted to share that sometimes we grab for things we cannot handle. I wanted to share that we must be willing to let go of things we can't handle. I wanted to share that sometimes our burdens become heavy and we need a helping hand. I could only imagine how I could have delivered a totally different presentation in that instant—all because my friend willingly helped to carry the cross. I shall always remember my friend and how his kind deed encouraged me, strengthened me, and revealed to me how God can send us help ***and*** meet our needs even before we ask. This, my friends, is just tip of the iceberg of what God can do with one thought or one deed—or one person!

Days later I gave television interviews and performed several of my songs, hoping my memory would serve me well for the lyrics. In addition, I later shared testimonies about my vehicle accident at different events and also ministered at several different churches. As I visited a senior citizen site and gave my testimony, one of the attendees said: *"Here I was at home praying for you and crying over your situation. And there you were in the hospital going to restaurants, going to the library, getting your hair done, and having fun."* We all laughed—but, seriously, it seems I was at peace and doing all of those things while confined to my hospital bed.

When people noticed my improved health, several of them came to me for advice when they were facing major upheaval in their lives, such as redundancy or courtship. Various ministry endeavors kept my mind flourishing. There were a few times, however, when I questioned whether I adequately vocalized my thoughts because of the earlier brain injury and associated memory problems. Sometimes I felt head discomfort and felt somewhat insecure that I was perhaps speaking unintelligibly. I could remember long-term details, but had a problem with short-term facts. There were times I did not recall what I had eaten or whether I had used the restroom on a given day. I would look at the faces of people I knew, but did not recall their names. In fact, I looked into the face of the man who introduced my husband to me, but could not remember the man's name. I called every man's name I knew, but still missed it. He gave me hint after hint, and eventually had to give me his initials for me to remember his name. That was a challenge for me indeed.

While relaxing one day, I had the opportunity to review our household financial status and concluded some adjustments were necessary. I shared my findings with my husband and we reached a consensus to streamline the monthly bills. One of the things I cancelled was a cancer insurance policy that was rather pricey for our budget. Several months thereafter, I felt lumps in my breasts. The first mammogram reports left me optimistic. Then six months later the results reflected some questionable abnormalities and the doctor recommended a biopsy. Immediately, I had thoughts that were not lining up with God's word. Negative ideas saturated my mind. While the biopsies results were being processed, I frequently thought about the insurance policy that I had already cancelled. Thank God the results were *benign*. Just one year later, however, the mammogram is again *abnormal*. What is going on? Is my faith being tested again? Surely, I had to believe, I serve the same God who healed my body and restored my health from the vehicle accident; He can heal my body from any disease (Psalm 103:3). God searches the heart and rewards us according to the actions we take by faith. I believed God's word and, sure enough, the Cancer Center again said the lumps in my breasts were *benign*. What a mighty God we serve.

I don't remember the accident; likewise, I don't recall ascending and descending into a heavenly realm as many other patients might describe. I know many times I have prayed, "Thy will be done on earth as it is in Heaven." **I believe Heaven came down to me on earth.** I was given therapy by angelic beings during the night. It seems angelic support was helping me to move body parts at night that human therapists could not help me to move during my day therapy. As I awoke during the night to exercise and strengthen my body with the angels, I felt empowered and was ready to show off in front of the human therapist. The day therapist kept commending me for my accelerated progress. God taught me during the night.

> *"It is good for me that I have been afflicted; that I might learn thy statutes"* (Psalm 119:71).

> *"Let the redeemed of the* LORD *say so, whom he hath redeemed from the hand of the enemy"* (Psalm 107:2).

Death had its chance at me, but lost during that vehicle accident. I know this world is not my home. My heavenly home is not made by man. I know I must die in order to live again and inhabit my mansion in the sky. No one is exempted from the clutches of death. One of my friends said she is grateful because she is *"still vertical and ventilated."* Likewise, I am also grateful. However, I have stared death in the face and lived to share my testimony. My near-death experience has caused me to reappraise my spiritual walk with God and become more loving and considerate of those around me. I have so much love to share with everyone now—I had to come back. My life was not finished.

Sometimes things seem to mysteriously enter our lives. Jesus did not prevent His disciples from going through the storm, and neither did He avert the storm from me. After many storms in my life, the sun ultimately shined again. God had mercy on me and allowed His angels to protect me. You may have heard about me or what I have been through, but you don't know what God is bringing me *to*. Some have likened me to a well-known television teacher and I receive that honor in Jesus' name—but I want to be like Jesus! It is such an honor to receive and delve into the things of God as I contemplate the ministry assignment for my life. I have been through the fire and have been purified. I have come forth as pure gold. It is my turn, my time, and my season.

> *"But he knoweth the way that I take:* when *he hath tried me, I shall come forth as gold"* (Job 23:10).

> *"But many* that are *first shall be last; and the last* shall be *first"* (Matthew 19:30).

I know I am not the only person who has experienced physical and mental challenges in life. Yet I am the only person who can legitimately explain my own pain and process of healing. I told the doctors about my pain, and with their prodigious knowledge, they prescribed the cocktail to help alleviate the pain—but God did the healing. Some of my greatest pain did not come from my vehicular accident, but from the hurt I experienced in the church. I yearned to be accountable and submissive to leadership, but those were the people who misused and abused me. They were the ones who took my meekness for weakness. Sometimes, it seems, I just don't fit in anywhere. It seems everyone wants you to join something before they accept you as a gift to bless the church.

I acknowledge my own inadequacy and God's absolute adequacy to sustain my life. God tells me when to jump and I know He will catch me right on time. What a sigh of relief to know that I don't have to doubt—I CAN TRUST GOD! God can be trusted, even though at times things seem chaotic and results seem hidden. It is incumbent upon us to share God's goodness. God will help us to understand His word through His Holy Spirit. It is the Holy Spirit living in me who helps me do what I am doing. Holy Spirit is that living power working through us.

No matter how things look or what people say, God has the last word. Let God have the last word over your life so that you can live your life with a sense of purpose and meaning. Your life is precious. With God, *NOTHING IS IMPOSSIBLE*, and I come into agreement with you now, in Jesus' Name for great things in your life. It is hoped that you can use my story to encourage someone else. Furthermore, it is hoped that your faith in God stays intact. God gives us free will to make choices, so I encourage you to *choose this day who you will serve.* **Jesus is my Choice!**

After all the things I have endured, I am better prepared to minister to the needs in the Body of Christ. I want to see reproduced in others the things God has produced in me. Rehearsing my painful encounters may seem nebulous in contrast to my many blessings. The pains themselves have proven to be a blessing. Metaphorically, dirt was thrown on me, but only roses came forth. There are some things we *guess* in life and there are some things we *KNOW*.

Spiritual Observation Number 1 (Hospital and Church Comparisons):

Sometimes I wish I could go back to the day of the accident and ask some medical questions and understand the answers when they are provided. Unfortunately, there are many things in life that we will not understand. At one point, I was not able to ask any questions—I couldn't talk.

And even if I were able, I would not know the appropriate questions to ask about medical procedures. I am not a doctor and definitely could not tell the doctors and surgeons how to do their jobs. Neither my husband nor I could even read the doctors' notes. Though the doctors were attending to my body, my assumptions were predicated on the belief that the doctors were providing ultimate treatment. We trusted the doctors.

In the same way, we may not understand the entire Bible. We may not know all the questions to ask. There are probably some questions we don't even know how to ask. Yet we want to fistfight people about the Bible before we believe it or trust it. We are not smart enough to tell God how to manage the world and His creation. But we must trust God—just like we trusted those doctors. Doctors informed my husband of the possibility of paralysis, coma, additional surgeries, and even possible death, before they performed procedures. Likewise, Jesus has already informed us of obstacles and oppositions we will face in this life for following Him and the honor received in the end is life eternal with Him. Jesus tells us to *take up our cross* and follow Him. We must trust Him.

I also noticed how the medical staff worked masterfully as a team to care for my needs. Today I am walking in my healing as a result. Likewise, when the Body of Christ can use this analogy of teamwork to bring healing to those who are struggling in sin, we will foster healing in the church. It is our combined actions that help make up the reputation of the Body of Christ. No one knows everything, but we can learn something from each other and be supportive to promote collective goals. Each medical person had an assignment and each of them knew what to do at the right time. The nurses did not perform my surgeries, but their skills were vital to get the job done. They had extraordinary passion, intellect, and people skills to help others. The medical team had a plan to help me live and restore me to health, not to hurt me. Doesn't that sound like God's plan?

Anything's Possible: The 47-Day Prophecy

"For I know the thoughts that I think toward you, saith the Lord, thoughts of peace, and not of evil, to give you an expected end" (Jeremiah 29:11).

Spiritual Observation Number 2 (Premonitions):

- I unknowingly separated and pre-arranged my identification cards for easy retrieval for emergency medical staff and highway patrolmen.
- I prepared my bedroom on the day of the accident for my return 47 days later.
- I gave Shirley Davis the correct cell phone number to contact my husband about the accident and then collapsed.
- I was alert and talking intelligibly by the time I got to the emergency room. I told them which medicine I was allergic to and then collapsed *again*.
- Text messages were blasted to certain people from my cell phone number on the night of John-Michael's death while I was in the trauma unit.
- Email messages were blasted to my entire contact list on the night of John-Michael's death while I was in the trauma unit.
- I left a voice message at a business and asked the contact to call my house, not the hospital. The party called home and left a message for my husband that my call was being returned. I was just weaned from a coma—how did I remember the business telephone number? Why did I request that the party call my home? Upon my return home, I found out this incident worked for my good.

- I told Mary Canteen I dreamt one of my friend's sons was murdered and that she had three sons, instead of two. In actuality, I have two biological sons, but raised three boys. John-Michael, the third boy I raised, was in a fatal vehicle accident and died during the time of the dream episode. (I saw details—was it suicide or murder?)
- I saw an auditorium full of people and most of them were dressed in black. Was that John-Michael's funeral?
- I dreamt beforehand that I was administered duplicate medication and it happened soon afterward the same day.
- I was enthralled by the information I received through revelation.

I thank God for my spiritual recovery. My latter end is better—restoration, wholeness! Now I *know* God's glory.

"It is good for me that I have been afflicted; that I might learn thy statutes" (Psalm 119:71).

"Many are the afflictions of the righteous: but the Lord delivereth him out of them all" (Psalm 34:19).

"Though I walk in the shadow of death I will fear no evil…" (Psalm 23:4).

"Surely he hath borne our griefs, and carried our sorrows: yet we did esteem him stricken, smitten of God, and afflicted. But he was wounded for our transgressions, he was bruised for our iniquities: the chastisement of our peace was upon him; and with his stripes we are healed" (Isaiah 53:4-5).

"Who his own self bare our sins in his own body on the tree that we, being dead to sins, should live unto righteousness: by whose stripes ye were healed" (1 Peter 2:24).

"The Lord is on my side; I will not fear: what can man do unto me?" (Psalm 118:6).

"Why art thou cast down, O my soul? And why art thou disquieted within me? Hope thou in God: for I shall yet praise him, who is the health of my countenance, and my God" (Psalm 42:11).

"Despise not prophesying" (I Thessalonians 5:20).

"And it shall come to pass afterward, that I will pour out my spirit upon all flesh; and your sons and your daughters shall prophesy, your old men shall dream dreams, your young men shall see visions" (Joel 2:28).

"He that receiveth a prophet in the name of a prophet shall receive a prophet's reward; and he that receiveth a righteous man in the name of a righteous man shall receive a righteous man's reward" (Matthew 10:41).

"For the prophecy came not in old time by the will of man: but holy men of God spake as they were moved by the Holy Ghost" (2 Peter 1:21).

"The secret things belong unto the LORD our God: but those things which are revealed belong unto us and to our children for ever..." (Deuteronomy 29:29).

"If any man speak, let him speak as the oracles of God; if any man minister, let him do it as of the ability which God giveth: that God in all things may be glorified through Jesus Christ, to whom be praise and dominion for ever and ever. Amen" (I Peter 4:11).

"Many will say to me in that day, Lord, Lord, have we not prophesied in thy name? and in thy name have cast out devils? and in thy name done many wonderful works? And then will I profess unto them, I never knew you: depart from me, ye that work iniquity" (Matthew 7:22-23).

"For I am God, and there is none else; I am God, and there is none like me, Declaring the end from the beginning…My counsel shall stand, and I will do all my pleasure…I have spoken it, I will also bring it to pass; I have purposed it, I will also do it" (Isaiah 46:9-11).

"Behold, the former things are come to pass, and new things do I declare: before they spring forth I tell you of them" (Isaiah 42:9).

"When a prophet speaketh in the name of the LORD, if the thing follow not, nor come to pass, that is the thing which the LORD hath not spoken, but the prophet hath spoken it presumptuously: thou shalt not be afraid of him" (Deuteronomy 18:22).

"I have heard what the prophets said, that prophesy lies in my name, saying, I have dreamed, I have dreamed. How long shall this be in the heart of the prophets that prophesy lies? yea, they are prophets of the deceit of their own heart; Which think to cause my people to forget my name by their dreams…The prophet that hath a dream, let him tell a dream; and he that hath my word, let him speak my word faithfully… Behold, I am against them that prophesy false dreams, saith the LORD, and do tell them, and cause my people to err by their lies, and by their lightness; yet I sent them not, nor commanded them: therefore they shall not profit this people at all, saith the LORD.…I will even punish that man and his house" (Jeremiah 23:25-34).

Chapter Three

Pleasant Dreams

"And he said, Hear now my words: If there be a prophet among you, I the LORD will make myself known unto him in a vision, and will speak unto him in a dream" (Numbers 12:6).

Many people think everyone who is sedated and injured have strange dreams. While many individuals who have been in a medically induced coma experience horrific dreams that does not mean all of the patients do. Though some dreams are humorous and some full of mysteries, I am blessed to say that God used many of my dreams as a teaching ministry for me. God can speak mysteries to us through dreams and visions just as He did in ancient days. I don't claim to possess any clairvoyant talents or abilities, but I do believe in the power of God. I know that dreams are an enigma for many people. Dreams are not strange to me because I know God has enjoined dreams to help perpetuate life in me. Although I talk with a southern accent, I have had dreams about my heavenly vernacular. Words I heard spoken through my dreams assure me that some things I saw were attributed to neither hallucinations nor my medication. I don't recall any special television shows or radio programs that induced the content of my dreams. God instructs, teaches, and guides using whatever method He chooses. Some scriptures for further study about dreams are recorded in Joel 2:28 and Job 33:14-18.

God even spoke to the Apostle Paul through visions on several occasions (Acts 16:6-10; Acts 18:8-11, and Acts 22:17-21). Let us remember, though, that we are not to rely on dreams, visions, angelic visitation, or ministers and fail to read and study God's word. Anything that contradicts or fails to line up with God's word must be avoided. Have you had any dreams lately?

We must all acknowledge and agree with God's method in everything we do or say and know that He directs our path. No matter our talents, God wants our hearts! God's peace exceeds our understanding and will keep our hearts and minds through Christ Jesus. God helps us, strengthens us, and upholds us. He only asks that we trust Him and do not fear. God assures us of miracles and even accounted for His promises in the written word, the Bible. We can trust God to fulfill His word. God will help us, even through our dreams.

There are some amazing biblical stories of how God dealt with some of His people through dreams. I thought about how Joseph, one of the sons of Israel, encountered some major changes in his life as a result of his dream. Even a Pharaoh had a dream about Sarah being Abraham's wife, instead of his sister. And what about how Joseph had to make changes in his life because of a God-inspired dream to protect their baby, Jesus the Christ!

I have experienced nightmares that seemed unbelievably vivid and detailed. For all practical purposes, I won't share all of my dreams and visions while hospitalized because some of them were *for my eyes and ears only*. Sometimes I had lucid dreams or visions while my eyes were wide open. Read these scriptures and notice the power of God with visions as recorded in Numbers 12:6 and 1 Corinthians 14:31. Has God shown you anything lately? If I shared everything God showed me while I was in the hospital, no one would really try to understand me—they would only cheer me on. Several instrumental key elements opened my eyes and taught wisdom sessions for my greater ministry assignments. Yes, I saw images, but I don't recall any strange audible voices! I realize I had bleeding on my brain and was also heavily sedated at times. I know that I hallucinated at times and sometimes my dreams were elusive. At the same time, however, Holy Spirit, through His wisdom, ministered to and through me immensely. I know Holy Spirit was moving in my life in a mighty way during my hospital stay. Why is it that I remember all of these intense dreams and cannot remember that I was in a near-fatal accident? By the grace of God, I have experienced life-altering dreams. While hospitalized, not all of my lucid dreams can be attributed to hallucinations caused by sedating medication or to my brain hemorrhage. I have learned how to see things that God shows me even while I am asleep. I have a relationship with my Father and am learning to recognize His voice. I have learned over the years that a God-given message may seem as nonsense to an uninterested party. I included a few dreams that I had prior to the accident just to validate that I received messages through dreams before the brain injury. I will talk about a few of my dreams that may appear as foolishness to some, but I am able to get a message from each one of them. Though lying flat on my back in the hospital, God still trusted me to whisper in my ear—not my fleshly ear—but my spiritual ear. My phenomenal dreams offered encouragement and gave me wisdom, insight, and spiritual direction.

Who Is Teaching Our Children

I had an alarming dream prior to my vehicle accident in which grown men were inciting our children to use profanity. The naïve men disingenuously engaged the youth with appealing activities to lure them and earn their trust. Later, the men would have all the newly recruited children face the adults while new profane words were drilled in their heads; there were no word restrictions. The adults were participating in activities that were absolutely reprehensible and unacceptable. There are tantalizing clues that our youth are being deceived about the true meaning of life and that their lives matter. Whether we believe it or not, the enemy is using those we least expect to destroy our future leaders. Different media outlets are reinforcing this obscenity upon our youth. We have never before heard such vulgar language from young people as we witness today! The youth need to know that manners will take them a long way in life. Unfortunately, many people stop dead in their tracks when they decide to use etiquette only during emergency situations. We must be careful who our children associate with and teach them to avoid those who are known for such ill repute. Such is the case when we respect others only when we need something from them. To me, this was more than a dream, it was a premonition! Just as the Israelites did, it seems we, too, have forgotten to teach our children about *WHO* really matters the most—God!

The Dark Tunnel

In October 2012, prior to my accident, I experienced being in a dark capsule that seemed to have ascended faster than the speed of light. I actually felt the pressure from the speed. I said within myself, *you made it in.* But, at the same time, I did not see my husband or my sons in the place where I landed. It was my prerogative to find my family and ensure they had made it safely also. This was a joyous time for me, but I wanted to find my family. It seems like all of a sudden I dropped back into my body. Did I die during the night and was sent back to earth to witness to my family. My heart was racing really fast and my head felt like I had just exited a roller coaster. I got out of bed, staggering and looking for my husband. He was awake in the den and watching the television. I told him, *"Something happened to me. I thought the world had ended."* My husband said, *"You just dreamt about something you heard on the news about the world ending in October 2012."* I felt the urge to walk away from a potential fight, despite my husband's provocation over the matter. I kindly turned around and went back to my bed, wondering what had just happened to me in the tunnel. This was not a dream! What happened to me?

Family Matters

Family is of utmost importance to me. It is said, *"Blood is thicker than water."* Yet there are many families that are torn apart for one reason or another. I am no exception to the travesty that permeates the home life of those who are serious about maintaining happy and healthy relationships. Even though I love people, especially my family, it is heartbreaking when I hear of division among families who confess the name of Jesus Christ. People loved each other even before Jesus was born. Yet He said "a new commandment" about love. Moses said, *"Love your neighbor as yourself"* (Leviticus 19:18). Then Jesus presented an update and said, Love *"as [God] has loved you"* (John 13:34). Oh, how God loves me! His standard is so high until it seems we should never feel we have loved someone *too* much. Real Christians are identified by their love.

While hospitalized, I dreamt about one of my half-sisters who disowned me as her sister. She really weighed heavily in my heart. In real life, I had made several attempts to rectify our relationship, but to no avail. I don't condone the nonsense that I see happening that pulls families apart. Therefore, the dream was dreadfully disturbing, but at the same time it was uplifting. I was still disoriented, but the dream seemed so real! I awoke and shared some information with my nurse that she deemed important enough to log in my medical file. In my mind, I had hospitably invited my sister to have breakfast with me at the hospital. I kept asking the nurse, *"Is she here yet?"* Being fully awake at this point, it appeared that my hospital monitoring equipment had reverted to modern communication technology. It seemed my nurse's call button was a remote controller for the equipment and I could answer the phone with a touch of a button. All of this was surreal. I had public officials calling me, including the sheriff, informing me of a live radio broadcast that my sister would be hosting. I presumably tuned in to the broadcast and heard a live radio interview as my half-sister publicly announced that *"Evelyn Murray Drayton is indeed my sister."*

When my sister did not show up for breakfast in my room, I resorted to writing her a letter. Even on my sick bed, I scribbled a letter to my sister. Along with many misspelled words, the essence of the letter stated that *"It took twenty-plus years for you to own me and I am so glad you had a change of heart."* I asked *the nurse* to type the lengthy letter for me. The nurse insisted that I rewrite the letter and hand deliver it to my sister upon her arrival to my room. With each rewrite (three attempts) of the letter, my handwriting and cognitive skills improved. I thought my final handwritten copy was perfect, but it was strikingly illegible (I didn't know it though). The nurse neglected typing my letter, so, this time, I requested that she fax my handwritten letter. The nurse said she didn't have the fax number. I told her that my sister was a councilwoman and they could easily find her office number in the telephone book. I know this nurse had to be livid with me by then! The nurse tricked me and stamped a big red **"FAX"** on my letter and handed it back to me. I had bothered this nurse so much about the letter until tricking me was probably the best way to appease me. I was so thankful and peaceful when I knew the letter had been faxed. I even told some of my visitors that I had written and faxed a letter to my sister. I saved the original copy of the letter that was **supposedly faxed** to my sister. I did not know the nurse tricked me until about a month after my hospital release—**duh**! I guess I appeared to be an ineffectual fool! But I had heard that the *"squeaky wheel gets the grease!"* There was a lot of rigmarole in the dream and also in my conscious mind. However, my dream was significant because this sister has never acknowledged that I am related to her. To me, God gave me peace through my dream. *How did I remember all of this with bleeding on the brain?*

Conniving Nurses

The doctors had performed a tracheotomy and had to remove the tubes within a set number of days to prevent vocal cord injuries. I assume this medical apparatus was atrociously uncomfortable. And, yes, I did the same thing many other patients are forever doing—I unknowingly pulled out my trach tube, which doctors had to reconnect. This all happened about the same time doctors were weaning me out of the induced coma. My nephew, **Johnny Leon Murray**, who visited me from North Carolina, told me this incident happened during the time he was in my room, but I was unaware of his presence. He said the medical staff immediately ushered him out of my room because I became agitated and pulled the lines and leads from my body. It was one of the most egregious mistakes I could have made, but let me tell you my reason for pulling the tube. I dreamt one of the nurses had misapplied something on my tube and conspired with another nurse to cover up the mistake. In the dream, it seems I had manually—but secretly—pulled the tube and corrected the problem myself. The conspiracy was only a dream—but I had detached the tube for real, which required a reinstallation. The dream was surreal! Later on, during my recovery, one of the nurses asked me why I disconnected the tube. I didn't want to tell the nurse the dream about the conspiracy theory. But who knows if that was God's way of working out a problem for my good, huh?

In another dream, my doctor prescribed an experimental drug for me, but the entire test initially yielded unfavorable results. It appeared my medication was ineffective due to a devious nurse's scheme to skew the test results. This plotting does not fit the modus operandi of such a great group of nurses. This conniving nurse had sabotaged minutiae of the specialist who was designated to administer the test. I informed the test administrator that someone, this culprit, was tampering with my medication. I was appalled by this behavior, but I had no one to corroborate my story. Medical personnel surreptitiously set up a camera and monitored the activities of the scheming nurse through their one-way mirror. The nurse would innocently enter my room and immediately look around furtively as she headed toward the medical syringe. Hospital security squelched the nefarious goings-on as the nurse concocted her ingredients, one of which was later identified as *iodine*. This caused great exasperation among all those who viewed the video. After this ploy was thwarted, I received optimum patient care and my specialist was able to record remarkable improvement in my health.

Ultimate Deception—All For the Love of Money

Social media has taken over the one-on-one contact to which many people are accustomed. Although I would like to expurgate some verbal and visible images from social media, God allows many good and timely words to flow from those gates. Nonetheless, while hospitalized, I dreamt of an ultimate social media deception in progress. It seemed one of the nurses registered me on a social site that portrayed me as a woman of questionable character, flaunting flamboyant apparel. The nurse's husband became disappointed with the derogatory and sexually explicit comments that men had registered on my profile. He monitored the high rating on the site and recommended that his wife, the nurse, close the account. He told his wife that such promotion was out of character for me and that I did not need that type publicity. It gave me satisfaction to know the site would be shut down because of this man's observation and consideration for my reputation. Unfortunately, the conceited nurse inwardly celebrated the site's high rating because she was getting paid for each registered click and comment on my site. The fact still remains that my reputation was at stake and we all know there is no anonymity on the World Wide Web. Initially, it appeared the nurse conceded and would disengage herself from the promiscuous mindset. Unbeknown to her husband and me, she manipulated the profile and continued to profit from the site. What a deception…all for the love of money!

<u>Church Imprisonment</u>

In this dream, I recognized the faces of a high-ranking church official, along with other clergy, in a very crowded restaurant. Some of those clergy had insidiously schemed against me. As I sought hopelessly for a table, that illustrious church official talked with the other clergy then looked at me and said, "*I got you now.*" Needless to say, but I will say anyhow, there is a lot of jealousy and power struggle in God's house. I recall how church leaders in Jesus' day were jealous when they saw the crowd following Jesus. Some of the same foolishness is rampant in God's house today. How is it that ministers invite me to schools, hospitals, and jails, but won't invite me in ***their*** church pulpit? I understand that leaders are to be careful about who is feeding their flock and what is being fed to the flock. Many leaders need to acknowledge, though, that it may be some of their unrelenting foolishness that contributes to the high church attrition rate.

The Holy Spirit impressed upon my heart that I am a *billboard* for Kingdom purpose. A billboard does not have to make a sound. It only needs to be placed where it can be seen. God is placing me where He needs me, so the only thing I really need to do is stand tall and be obedient. God uses me to communicate with the public as I catch people's attention, provide them spiritual information, and offer Jesus to them. He does it in such a way that people are left with a memorable impression of God's presence. Church officials see the hand of God over my life, but many ministers have intentionally attempted to close doors in my face. Where is the threat—who wants to usurp their authority? Does closing doors sound like they are fighting against me or against GOD? I know that I am not the only minister who has the Holy Ghost abiding on the inside by faith. God gives gifts to the church, but we must all work together to accomplish God's purpose. I think this

Scripture will fit here because when God opens doors, no other clergy can close those doors. Ask David, ask Jesus:

> *"And the key of the house of David will I lay upon his shoulder; so he shall open, and none shall shut; and he shall shut, and none shall open"* (Isaiah 22:22).

One leader insinuated that the assumption among several others was that I sought to build a church and **steal** their members. I don't need members in order to obey God. It is God who draws people to Himself anyhow. The reason many leaders are watering down the word of God is to increase funding and church membership. These types of goings-on can yield a *full* populated building with an *empty* heart for God's word. Furthermore, some leaders are so overly concerned about power (authority and control) until they refuse to allow the God-given spiritual gifts to operate in their churches. There is no need to masquerade ourselves as angels of light, knowing that we are full of pervasive darkness! Oh, yes, God showed me your faces!

If we are not careful, people will subjugate and imprison us while trying to serve *inside* the church. I am thinking about an out-of-town church visitation one Sunday where an elderly pastor and his wife were the only other two people in attendance. I still don't understand why I drove so far to be in service with only two people. But I believe it was a teaching and eye-opening moment for me. The pastor expressed his gratitude for my fellowship with them. I am not a musician, but as they sang, I volunteered to make a slightly off-key sound on their keyboard to help the service. They were so grateful for my *joyful* noise unto the Lord. After service the pastor said he believed the Lord sent me to join his church. I said, *"Well, I need to pray about that for myself!"* because I felt I was there only to encourage them, not to join. Then the pastor invited my children and me to dinner at one of their local restaurants. While we were parting ways, the pastor said, *"I can certainly use your service and you will be a blessing to the church. If you don't feel you should be a member of my church, don't come back."* I was not intimidated by any means and had concluded that the leader's attitude was probably the reason no others had been in their church fellowship. I was devastated to hear those words coming from someone who represents Christ and immediately recognized that God was not speaking. It seems some leaders think people need to beg them to be a member of their church. Rather, it should be a privilege and an honor for someone to choose a given place of worship that is under your leadership. As you probably figured, I did not return for another visit. I sat ruminating on this event because I am becoming more attuned to the ways of God. I am noticing more church people manipulating others in order to fulfill their agenda—and their quota. I can see more clearly the people's hidden motives as well as the plan of God as my mind is progressively being fully restored.

    Some church people have a propensity toward entertainment during their assembly—something I don't have time for. I reminded myself that I don't have to be known and that everything is not noteworthy. People were drawn to my life as they witnessed God's miraculous healing power in my life. Things were looking good and doors of opportunities were speedily opening. Some people declared that my testimony shook them out of their complacency. I have a testimony now that many others probably experienced but did not live to tell. It was interesting to see how my calendar became filled again after my recovery. I had to get past *why* this happened to me and thank God for the privilege to see His healing power manifested in me and through me. I can attest to the words of the Shunammite woman (II Kings 4:26) when she expressed, *"All is well."* Now I have a new purpose in life. I try to encourage others and let them know that if they maintain a positive attitude and stay focused, they can better appreciate their recovery process and healing.

The Names of Two Boys

I shared this dream, every minute detail, with several of my visitors because I thought it actually happened—but it was only in my dream! One night I dreamt a nurse came to my bedside and said: *"Mrs. Drayton, I know you are a woman of God and I want you to tell me the names of my two boys."* I said, *"Tell you what?"* The nurse did not disclose if she was pregnant with twins, already had two boys, or whether she had planned to adopt two boys. I had never experienced such a spiritual challenge like that in my entire life. The nurse did not give me any details or even a clue about her family—not even initials for the two boys. When I appeared baffled, the nurse put some money that she called a *seed offering* under a bandage on my right thigh and said she knew God would give me the answer. She then exited my room.

Maybe this was a *dream within a dream*, but it seems I could not go to sleep after hearing the nurse's request. I stayed awake a long time contemplating the response for the nurse's question. When the nurse re-entered my room and saw that I was restless, she told me to go to sleep. Suddenly, God gave me the answer! And I knew that I knew God had given me the answer. The next morning I wrote the names **Peter** and **Obadiah** on a piece of paper and handed it to the nurse. When the nurse saw these names, she was flabbergasted! I looked at her apprehensively while trying to figure out what was happening to her. The nurse immediately telephoned her husband and her mother-in-law and told them about the names I gave her. They confirmed that the two names were identical names prophesied to them by her mother-in-law during prayer. So the nurse already knew the boys' names were Peter and Obadiah before she asked me. She was seeking another confirmation from the Lord to corroborate an adoption.

Later, I saw the nurse negotiating and signing the final adoption papers for the two Spanish-speaking boys—it was official! After the signing, the boys' biological mother entered my room in the dark to get a cold soda and noticed that I was still awake. Speaking English fluently, she said: *"You just don't know what you have done! Thank you."* The boys' mother was so amazed how God had moved on her behalf by placing her children with a loving family who would take good care of them. After the boys' mother met me, she and the nurse agreed that they would deposit a financial blessing in my bank account to express their appreciation. It seems the nurse scanned my hospital wristband to confirm my bank account number for the deposit. While I was still dreaming, the nurse told me she scheduled a meeting so that I could share my testimony about how God gave me the two boys' names. After that night-shift nurse was relieved, I asked the morning-shift nurse about the meeting because no one showed up at the scheduled time to hear my testimony. This nurse didn't have a clue what I was talking about.

I was so amazed that God had given me such spiritual revelation in my dream. I told a number of my visitors how God gave me the names of my nurse's two boys. I did not know it was all a dream. *It seemed so real.* I actually told people about the episode even after I was released from the hospital and was recuperating at home. As a matter of fact, the dream was so real that I checked my bank statement for confirmation of the nurse's bank deposit after I was released from the hospital. Yes, I did that!

Several members of my former church family from Davis Station, South Carolina, visited and I warmly shared my testimony about Peter and Obadiah with them. I did not know at the time it was only a dream—it was so real to me. When two of my precocious half-brothers visited, I also shared my testimony with them. They suggested that I look for a special message from **Peter** and **Obadiah** since these are names of two books in the Bible. Peter is from the New Testament and Obadiah is in the Old Testament. One of my brothers asked if I knew the meaning of the names Peter and Obadiah. I told him Peter means *rock*, but I didn't know anything about Obadiah. Weeks after I left the hospital, I shared my story with another relative who asked me to tell her about Obadiah. I didn't know what to say, so I immediately grabbed my Bible and found out that Obadiah speaks a lot about family matters. So, my relative, Cheryl, told me to *be encouraged about any family dissension and just stand on the ROCK (Jesus)*.

I believe in real life that God has bestowed upon me gifts of the word of knowledge and prophecy, which are included in the nine gifts of the Holy Spirit. The gifts were activated while I was on my hospital bed, and when I transferred to HealthSouth for therapy, God manifested His power using those gifts to bless the people. I believe these and other gifts, such as healing, will make room for me as I manifest God's power and glory in ministering to the people. I thank God for increased financial acumen. Finances will flow as I flow and glow for my Heavenly Father. I wouldn't dare say that I serendipitously discovered these precious gifts. Nor will I give bleeding on the brain, medication, or hallucination the credit for lessons learned from this dream. Even though this revelation was instigated by a dream, Holy Spirit spoke to me during the dream and said, *"My people do not use half the power and authority I have given them."* Powerful!

No More Chipped Ice

I have to conjecture that Satan was attacking me in my dreams. The enemy gave his best shots and was determined to destroy me. My doctor gave explicit orders that the nurses withhold cold drinks and ice from me for a period of time when my tracheal tube was initially inserted. It seems I yearned for ice like a pregnant woman craves pickles and ice cream—just because they told me I couldn't have ice. I even tried to get ice by chewing on the sponge the nurse gave me to moisten my tongue. Did I think the sponge contained ice? The nurse scolded, *"Mrs. Drayton, you know better than to chew that sponge. Spit it out—don't swallow that sponge."* I wanted some ice in my mouth so bad I wanted to steal it. The enemy tried to use my desire for ice to entice me to *escape* from my bed during the night to find some chipped or crushed ice—this was a ploy to paralyze me. The enemy told me to steal some ice while the nurses were not watching and that it would be a while before they come to check on me. I started looking all over the room for water, for a water fountain, for ice cubes, for chipped ice. But, so plainly, Holy Spirit whispered to me and said, *"The nurses may not see you, but God would."* I immediately closed my eyes and repented that it was in my heart to steal ice. When the nurse came back to my room, I nonchalantly said, *"Please, ma'am, give me some ice."* The nurse said, *"Wait just a little while longer, Mrs. Drayton."* Sure enough, as time passed, I was able to *eat* all the ice I wanted. It all seemed so real. I learned that the enemy will try to pinpoint your desires and try to outwit you at your weakest point. The enemy wants you to crave those things that are not good for you in an effort to destroy you. Sometimes we just have to wait a little while and our needs will be met. Sometimes things are withheld from us for a period for our own good. Satan will tempt you to help satisfy your desires. Just thinking of the word *ice* increased my desire for ice. I wanted ice so bad that I was willing to steal it to satisfy a desire. What is it that Satan is trying to tempt you with? What is it that you want so bad you are willing to do wrong to get it? Think about it! Yes, God ministered to me and He taught me in my hospital room through dreams. No more chipped ice—God is watching, even when you think no one else is!

Blood Collection Hidden Agenda

I dreamt a new nurse, the face of a lady I recognized from Georgetown, reported for duty and befriended me. At first, it seemed there was a strong feeling of camaraderie. This nurse dressed me each day, making sure that I donned her *favorite color*. Even though she smiled with me, I detected an aura of deception around her. When she perceived that she could not recruit me for her sorority, she began treating me like a castaway. How could this sweet, loving lady treat me like a stray dog, even though I was a patient in the hospital and in need of loving care? Later, it seemed she, along with other sorores, was plotting a scheme to publicly embarrass and torment me. Although they were rather evasive, I recognized a number of people in the group and their behavior within their secret societies.

I also saw a young man that I actually know, who, in the dream, was working at the nurses' station as a desk clerk. This same young man served as a nursing assistant and was responsible for drawing blood and changing patients' clothing and bedding during emergency situations. The young man would secretly draw patients' blood and use the vials of blood for his fraternity and some other satanic purposes. It seems he foisted the blood collection several times, but later realized that I had detected his misdoings. As he ran amok, an entourage of ladies, who were nurses, donned regalia pertinent to their sororities while chanting some words over the collected blood. They were praying for some of the patients to become deathly ill to extend their hospital stay for blood collection—and some others they prayed would die. I felt the presence of evil and pled the blood of Jesus time after time. This was such a precarious situation, knowing they could make me suffer at their hands. I was in spiritual warfare right there on my hospital bed. There was a need for me to war with my tongue by speaking aloud the word of God. Tranquility overtook my room when I prayed and believed. God hears, heals, and He is available to help us. *"Let us therefore come boldly unto the throne of grace, that we may obtain mercy, and find grace to help in time of need"* (Hebrews 4:16).

While the young clerk manned the front desk, he heard me praying and detected that I was praying against their evil. He then asked if I wanted him to close my door—I said, *"No."* I was asked several times if I wanted my door closed and I relentlessly kept telling him the same thing. At one point, the young man told another nurse to ask me if I wanted my door closed. I informed her that I would let her know when to close my door. One particular nurse was the same face of a nurse who, presumably, gave me extra rectal suppositories, which resulted in my excessive stomach pain and extensive fecal testing at the Centers for Disease Control. The collusion leads one to believe that patients' lives or deaths are sometimes in the hands of conspirators. The dream was demonstrative of how possible lifelong implications occur when sick patients are cared for by sadistic medical personnel, or are cared for in a satanically induced environment. I saw nurses and other staff who converged to worship idol gods and performed despicable acts during the services. They attended worship services on their breaks and returned to care for patients, showing ambiguity of job duties.

    I never knew the importance of knowing how to plead the blood of Jesus to such a degree until I dreamt about the evil being concocted. There was disarray and it appeared that competition among sororities and fraternities was more important than working together for a common cause. It seemed rivalry superseded the good purpose for which the organizations were created. I learned that everyone who smiles in your face is not your friend. We must know that all medical workers are not Christians. I learned that people don't always have good motives for being nice to you. I learned that some people apply for certain jobs with a hidden agenda. I also learned that there are people in positions to care for others, but they will be the first to destroy the patient if their plan is interrupted. Again, not everyone who cares for patients is Christian.

Seminar Presentation

    I dreamt a seminar was held at the hospital, specifically in my room. It seemed the presenter wanted me to use the bedpan in front of her attendees, but I refused to do so. The presenter became irate because I disrupted the flow of her presentation by not using the bedpan for her openly. The presenter nevertheless charged the hospital a huge sum of money since the seminar did not go as she planned. One of the doctors later commended me for standing my ground. *This scene encouraged me to be bold and firm.*

In the other scene, it seemed this same lady, the presenter, served as one of my nurses and later spent a lot of time in my room trying to sell me some of her products for my breathing apparatus and tube feeding formula. On one occasion she wore a burgundy uniform, instead of the white, as she sampled her products to clean and deodorize my bathroom. Her meandering allowed her time to spray fumes in my room and insert medicine in my breathing machine. Her good-smelling products would be especially enticing if potential buyers could smell the refreshing fragrance that permeated my room. The nurse even presented some food products that could be used intravenously. She was upset when we chose the hospital products instead of the ones she tried to sell. But, with her products, my breathing improved and my overall health improved drastically. The lady told me that she would be able to supply her products after my hospital release as well. She even arranged a conference to further discuss her products and services with my husband and me. The lady was rather persuasive! The next morning, I asked my husband what he thought about the lady and her products. Russell said he didn't have a clue what I was talking about. Oh my goodness—another dream? Why the burgundy color? How could I smell the fragrance from the dream while I was awake? Why did my breathing improve the next day in real life just as revealed in the dream?

Family Accident Involving My SUV

I dreamt my family was involved in a vehicular accident as I drove my SUV to North Carolina to visit my oldest son, Justin. I told the patrolman there were five passengers inside my vehicle, including my grandchild. At the time, I didn't have a grandchild and desperately tried to find out how I had a grandchild in my vehicle. It seems someone told me my son had a baby with a girl from Hemingway, South Carolina, and the girl's mother's name was Mary. I thought of every Mary I knew in South Carolina, it seemed, but nothing registered. No one told me which one of my sons fathered the child. My husband then told me not to tell the patrolman there were five people in my vehicle. Anxiously, I told my husband that it was already public knowledge because a young man, a former coworker, read about my accident on the Internet. Upon Russell's visit the next morning, I told him there were five occupants in my vehicle and I could name the people. Russell tried hard to convince me that it was only a dream and that I was the sole occupant in my vehicle. Yet the dream seemed so real that I jabbered incessantly about other passengers who sustained injuries in my vehicle. As I recovered at home, I searched the Internet profusely in an attempt to find the news articles that I dreamt my former coworker had read. Fortunately, it was only a dream, because I found only news coverage about the deceased driver—nothing about me or my vehicle. I was still apprehensive about the five passengers until I read the official police report that verified I was the only person in my vehicle. Thank God there were no other injured people; it was only a dream. (*Now I wonder whether this dream had anything to do with John-Michael's death. Although I am John-Michael's aunt, when his son Jaysen was born, John told me I was a new "grandma." John was the fifth family member in my household before he moved away. But Jaysen's grandmother's name is not Mary, even though I really do have a friend named Mary who lives in Hemingway!*)

Who Killed John?

I dreamt about a former coworker and his family. In real life, they have only two sons. In the dream, however, they had three boys. The oldest of the three brothers had everyone fooled because of his excellent mannerisms and no one suspected he was involved in any mischievous activities. It seemed there was parental favoritism for the youngest son, named **John**, who had married a beautiful young woman and had moved into a nice big house. The oldest son, on the other hand, married someone who was not acceptable to his parents, so that increased animosity for his youngest brother. The oldest son plotted to kill John and succeeded in doing so. He paid a hit man to kill John because of his success. When all the dust settled, John was murdered out of pure jealousy and hatred. I cried, I cried, I cried! I woke up crying and a nurse asked me why I was so upset. I told her one of my friend's sons was murdered. As a matter of fact, later this same day I asked my friend, Mary Canteen, several questions about this family and their boys. Mary said she got a bit nervous because she knew she was not supposed to tell me that John-Michael was dead. She said I was asking questions as if I had already known—but I didn't know. *(Did this dream inform, warn, or confirm to me that John-Michael's death was homicide instead of suicide as reported?)*

I Want To Be at the Meeting

I'm debating whether or not this was a dream: I wanted to attend a meeting that I thought was being held in a room down the hall from my hospital room. There was a crowd of people in attendance. It seems it was a community meeting and some former business colleagues were in attendance. I believed if I could show up, these people would donate funds to my community. I didn't know that I was broken and battered and couldn't get out of bed. I was so adamant about attending that a nurse came up with a brilliant idea. The nurse told me if I allowed her to use my hospital bracelet, she would attend the meeting in my place. I wanted to go, but I allowed the nurse to scan my bracelet and go in my stead. (Wow, did she brilliantly trick me!) When the doctor entered my room, I told him about the meeting. He asked me why I wanted to attend the meeting. Of course, I repeated details about the need for my community donation. Anyhow, later in the day or the next day, I asked the nurse if any of the donors contributed to my community cause. The nurse told me, *"No."* Then I told her, *"That's exactly why I implicitly suggested attending the meeting for myself."* (Was I rude?) Although, I did not officially attend the meeting, I was still able to visualize the stage and see where certain people were seated. I scanned the audience and saw the people who I wanted to sit beside all dressed in black. I felt they knew me and would be influential in granting my request for funding. Before the meeting ended, I was back in my bed. Yet I heard and saw several of the attendees exiting the auditorium and heading to the hospital elevator. I heard the voices of those I chose to sit beside in the auditorium and thought they would stop by my room. It sounded as if a couple of them said they needed to get home before dark. I was disappointed when they never showed up to check on me. *(Was this crowd of people indicative of John-Michael's funeral?)*

Did My Angel Have the Face of a Relative?

I dreamt that a Drayton family member worked at the hospital and cared for me. Even though the family member did not provide medication, she made certain the nurses gave me special attention. She seemed to have been a dispatch operator or someone that reported the medical condition of patients en route to the hospital by way of ambulance. The dream was so vivid that when she visited me the next day, I complimented the burgundy uniform she wore the night before while working downstairs at the hospital. She looked at my husband as if to say, *"Yeah, Evelyn still has a little brain problem."* Well, I admit her employment at the hospital was only a dream. However, the dream showed me and assured me that **Shirley "Shirl" Drayton** of **Georgetown** has genuine love and is concerned about my well-being. In real life, I can always count on Shirl if I need a helping hand. After my release from the hospital she made certain I had adequate pillow cushions to support my broken hip. I thank God for her and all of my family members. *Did my angel watch over me in the hospital, using Shirl's face?*

Another Angel Checked On Me

I dreamt a former coworker's daughter came to the hospital and repaired my medical equipment. My nurse introduced the young lady to me, but was surprised that we already knew each other. I remembered the young lady before she graduated high school and was honored and grateful that she had matriculated college and was now able to help me. It seems she had traveled a distance to come to my room, but she was the only person in the surrounding area who was certified and knew the right codes to repair my equipment. As I turned my head slightly, I could see her husband standing near the doorway. He stuck his head into my room and said he was there only because he didn't want his wife traveling so far by herself that night. His sweet wife cautiously loaded some coded instructions into my equipment using her secret access codes. Hooray! The young lady fixed my equipment and said, *"Mrs. Evelyn, you are good to go. You will be fine now!"* God used these words for confidence and encouragement to help me during my recovery. Although I was motivated and liberated, I did not know this was only a dream. The dream seemed so real and I was so appreciative for the young lady's services. When I was released from the hospital, I called the young lady to express my thankfulness, but she informed me that she never visited the hospital. Yet she shared how she and other coworkers had met in an office to pray for my total recovery. What an awesome God we serve!

Dreaming Is a Blessing

Dreaming can reveal deep and, sometimes, surprising truths. It amazes me that I learned so much about myself and my surroundings through dreams. How is it possible that I recalled all of those detailed dreams? Were all of those dreams incited by or results of my trauma or medication? YOU KNOW BETTER! God is able to show us things, even through dreams, that seem almost unbelievable. I learned that God cleanses us before He strategically uses us. He wants us to examine ourselves, separate ourselves, and He will provide the revelation and exaltation that we need. He wants us to be effective witnesses of His love and who He is, thus winning other souls. We are to draw closer to God as we meet Him in that secret place. God's presence is that secret place and is where God gives you a heads up. Victory belongs to us if we stay in His presence and do not draw back from Him during adversities. Some people may wonder why I live the way I do. They may even wonder why I make the unpopular decisions that I make on certain matters. Well, sometimes I get a heads up from the secret place—even in my dreams! Some things we know the answers to; some things we try to search or figure out; some things are none of our business to know until or if God gives the revelation. There are Scriptures throughout the Bible that let us know God has some secret things which He shares with whomever He chooses (Deuteronomy 29:29; Daniel 2:22; Proverbs 25:2).

<u>Dreamer Beware</u>

I know we are peculiar and the Bible tells us so (I Peter 2:9). Sometimes others may believe we are physically stripped down to nothing, but God can beautifully redress us—even through the blessing of dreams. He can restore us physically and mentally for His purpose. I remember several of my *delusion*s, but have a hard time recalling the harsh realities of the auto collision. In the same way, some people may confuse God's voice with the harsh reality of other voices and mislead the masses. Many people have experienced disastrous results because some "spirit-led person" tells us, *God said*. After all our shared dreams, we must be careful not to deceive people and tell them **GOD** said when God did not say. Please read the scriptures below as a warning and also as an eyeopener:

> *20 "The anger of the Lord will not turn back until he fully accomplishes the purposes of his heart. In days to come you will understand it clearly. 21 I did not send these prophets, yet they have run with their message; I did not speak to them, yet they have prophesied. 22 But if they had stood in my council, they would have proclaimed my words to my people and would have turned them from their evil ways and from their evil deeds. 23 "Am I only a God nearby," declares the Lord, "and not a God far away? 24 Who can hide in secret places so that I cannot see them?" declares the Lord. "Do not I fill heaven and earth?" declares the Lord. 25 "I have heard what the prophets say who prophesy lies in my name. They say, I had a dream! I had a dream! 26 How long will this continue in the hearts of these lying prophets, who prophesy the delusions of their own minds? 27 They think the dreams they tell one another will make my people forget my name, just as their ancestors forgot my name through Baal worship. 28 Let the prophet who has a dream recount the dream, but let the one who has my word speak it faithfully. For what has straw to do with grain?" declares the Lord. 29 "Is not my word like fire," declares the Lord, "and like a hammer that breaks a rock in pieces? 30 "Therefore," declares the Lord, "I am against the prophets who steal from one another words supposedly from me. 31 Yes," declares the Lord, "I am against the prophets who wag their own tongues and yet declare, 'The Lord declares.' 32 Indeed, I am against those who prophesy false dreams," declares the Lord. "They tell them and lead my people astray with their reckless lies, yet I did not send or appoint them. They do not benefit these people in the least,"*

declares the Lord. 33 'When these people, or a prophet or a priest, ask you, What is the message from the Lord?' say to them, What message? I will forsake you, declares the Lord.' 34 If a prophet or a priest or anyone else claims, 'This is a message from the Lord,' I will punish them and their household. 35 This is what each of you keeps saying to your friends and other Israelites: 'What is the Lord's answer?' or 'What has the Lord spoken?' 36 But you must not mention 'a message from the Lord' again, because each one's word becomes their own message. So you distort the words of the living God, the Lord Almighty, our God. 37 This is what you keep saying to a prophet: 'What is the Lord's answer to you?' or 'What has the Lord spoken?' 38 Although you claim, 'This is a message from the Lord,' this is what the Lord says: You used the words, 'This is a message from the Lord,' even though I told you that you must not claim, 'This is a message from the Lord.' 39 Therefore, I will surely forget you and cast you out of my presence along with the city I gave to you and your ancestors. 40 I will bring on you everlasting disgrace— everlasting shame that will not be forgotten."
(Jeremiah 23:20-40 NIV)

"I have heard what the prophets said, that prophesy lies in my name, saying, I have dreamed, I have dreamed. How long shall this be in the heart of the prophets that prophesy lies? yea, they are prophets of the deceit of their own heart; Which think to cause my people to forget my name by their dreams…The prophet that hath a dream, let him tell a dream; and he that hath my word, let him speak my word faithfully… Behold, I am against them that prophesy false dreams, saith the LORD, *and do tell them, and cause my people to err by their lies"* (Jeremiah 23:25-32).

"Thus saith the LORD of hosts, Hearken not unto the words of the prophets that prophesy unto you: they make you vain: they speak a vision of their own heart, and not out of the mouth of the Lord" (Jeremiah 23:16).

"And it shall come to pass in the last days, saith God, I will pour out of my Spirit upon all flesh: and your sons and your daughters shall prophesy, and your young men shall see visions, and your old men shall dream dreams" (Acts 2:17).

"The Lord is on my side; I will not fear: what can man do unto me?" (Psalm 118:6).

Chapter Four

Power of Healing Words and Deeds

"It is not the one who speaks the loudest; it is more so the one who says the right words at the right time." E.M. Drayton

Hopeless and helpless conditions can be removed from our personal atmosphere. Yet, if we are not careful, we will allow other people to make us think God is not able to do the impossible. Are you grateful to be alive? Then let God know you are grateful! Would you like to be able to *speak* to an area in your life that needs healing and receive what you speak? Well, first of all, your words must line up with God's written word. Don't allow negative thoughts and words to dominate your life. Satan wants to label you and have others perceive you as coward, hypocrite, prideful, deceitful, and even judgmental. Don't entertain those derogatory remarks. There are many anointed people, but for some reason or other their attitudes are not pleasant. The unpleasant attitudes can adversely affect powerful testimonies that people need. We have to allow love to cover the bad attitudes. Although we are connected to people and their plans, we must not fail to realize it is about God, His plan, and His purpose. You may never fully understand what God is doing! We need to trust God and God wants people He can trust. Can God trust us to obey even when we don't understand? What deeds have we done for the Lord lately?

God's promises are so profound and defined that He has written them in the Bible. *"No sicknesses or injuries are greater than God's power"* (Mark 9:23). I believe in healing as well as God's other benefits and promises for His children. With God, all things are possible to us. **I have learned that God can take my obstacles and create opportunities.** With that said, I proclaim: ***I'm your "possibility expert"*** when discussing mental, physical, and emotional challenges. My near-death experience has really changed my life and my words. There are times I forget things, but Holy Spirit has a way of bringing words to my remembrance at the right time. We must ask *God* to help us with this tongue, which no *man* can tame. Out of the abundance of the heart the mouth speaks. Holy Spirit helps me to speak words that impact the lives of others to help them live more abundant lives! May my *purpose* for being alive prove not to be in vain! May Jesus shine through my life that others see more of **Him** than of me. Let the word of the Lord, not empty rehearsed words, flow freely through your lips. Don't allow the enemy to shut you up in his effort to shut you down. I refuse to follow Satan's plan for me to stay bruised and broken. These areas are on Satan's radar, but God has given us His Holy Spirit and His word as interceptors against Satan's plans. One of my favorite scriptures as an interceptor is Psalm 32:8: *"I will instruct thee and teach thee in the way which thou shalt go: I will guide thee with mine eye."* I trusted God to show me how to overcome my situation. You, too, can look and listen for the voice of the Lord, my friends.

I enjoy being in the presence of people with jovial personalities. I met many of my friends through my writing, music, and teaching ministries. One of my friends, **Dr. Sandra Carter Snyder of McClellanville, South Carolina**, came to my home and offered words of encouragement. She said, *"Evelyn, you're not a chicken—you're an eagle. Don't you forget that eagles travel alone, so don't you feel bad* *if anyone calls you a lone ranger. You are an eagle."* This reminds me that even though the Lone Ranger rode with Tonto, each man had his own horse. There were times they had to go separate ways and come together again later in order to accomplish their purpose. Dr. Snyder's words were powerful and timely for me because they encouraged me to stand, even when I have to stand alone.

My messages of hope, through books and songs, have ministered to many people, including myself, over the years. I first started my writing with the book, **I Had to Die Exposing Witchcraft in the Church**, which describes a church incident about which several of the members demanded that *I remain silent*. The pastor at that time told me if I exposed that he was practicing witchcraft he would bury me in 90 days. I told my story anyhow! It seems that at first no one wanted to believe my story that this church leader tried to kill me using witchcraft. He also tried to defame my character among many in the religious community. This church incident was a near-fatal experience for me. I learned quickly that not everyone who says he or she is sent to preach is actually a God-sent minister. While I respect most religious leaders, I nearly died at the hand of that evildoer. Although I was ostracized, Holy Spirit consoled me and I was victorious in the midst of it all.

My second book, titled **Silent Speaker**, has touched the hearts of many. It reminds me that God is watching over me. It also expounds on the church experience from my first book. Although it appeared to my finite mind that God had overlooked my maltreatment, He *was not silent*. God assured me that He speaks in ways that many people tend to ignore until offenders experience His wrath. God allowed me to place this book in various locations as a ministry tool. As a result, a young man, **James R. Glisson, Jr.**, affectionately called **Jamie**, of the Plantersville Section of Georgetown, read my book and shared the book with a few of his friends. Jamie wanted to bless my ministry by writing and mailing me three of his original poems. He gave me permission to use them in any way I choose. I chose to publish them right here in appreciation for God using my book *Silent Speaker* to touch his life:

The Castle of Hope

The castle of hope is standing afar
Many doors closed, but only a few ajar
I've opened the many and they led me astray
I've come back with faith to open the right one today
There are not many doors left open for me
I'm down to my final chances, so which will it be?
There are so many doors the Devil stands behind
Awaiting your choice so he can enter your mind
There is one and only one that can lead you away from sin
This is the Door to Heaven when you open it
Your life will then begin!
__ JRG, Jr. __

Footprints Continued

I saw your footprints again today
Then I saw the ocean sweep them away
I remember all the times you carried me
You opened my eyes, now I can see
I have a new favor of you to ask
Something small, a light little task
Father, will you carry me once again
I'm afraid this battle in me is one I can't win
Like the sea, what a beautiful sight
When you wrap your arms around me and hold me tight

Lately, it seems I've been walking alone
I try to do right but end up doing wrong
I'm on my knees crying out to you
I've seen your miracles; I know what you can do
I need another chance, just one more try
I've blown so many and I don't know why?
I've come today to ask you to forgive
I'm tired of dying, Father, I want to live
Thank you, Lord, for forgiving me
And giving me back the keys to Eternity.
— JRG, Jr. —

Home

Oh, what a beautiful sight
Driving down Highway 701 late at night
Going home to my family again
Oh, what a journey this has been
The stars are shining so bright
My road's coming up on the right
A few more miles and I'm there
To a home with the people I care
God you have done so much
When I stumbled you were my crutch
Home at last today's journey ends
Time to go call all my friends
Let them know I made it home
That I wasn't on this journey alone
God was with me the whole trip
Until I left, until I pulled back in my slip
Thank you, Lord, you're my best friend
Thank you for letting me see Plantersville once again.
— JRG, Jr. —

My book ***Feathered Wisdom*** shares how God used my early childhood years of farm experiences to prepare me for the oncoming years. My grandfather encouraged me to face fear and not run away from possible threats or challenges. ***Sweet Success After Bitter Defeat*** encourages me to stay focused and press forward. Even though my mind told me I was defeated during adversities, God shows me that I am still a success in His eyes. Now that I concur with God's assessment of my life, I am able to share in my book ***Watermelon Faith*** many of my lessons learned from various underhanded church-related incidents. The next book, ***Beyond Our Scars,*** shares how my many experiences do not deter me from climbing toward my destiny. It seems I experienced so much pain, heartache, and disappointments in life. However, I was able to move beyond those dreadful days and enjoy the sunshine in my life. The seventh book, ***AND SUDDENLY***, assures me that I have passed my spiritual self-recognition test. I have finally recognized who I am in Christ and who Christ is in me. I talk exhaustively about the gift of prophecy in that book. I refuse to allow promises for my life to dry up and die in my heart. And, suddenly, the promises of God are being manifested in my life as I learn more of Him and that He is indeed faithful to His word.

One of the songs I wrote and recorded, ***Don't Burn Down My Bridge,*** has been played on several radio stations and landed me a television spot in Atlanta, Georgia, on the **Babbie Mason Show** and **Preach The Word World Wide Network** in Tallahassee, Florida. Many people say the song reminds them of things they experienced in life, how they overcame, and how they are encouraged to keep pressing forward. Also, my song ***That's What Using Drugs Can Do*** landed me a spot on television in Atlanta, Georgia, as well. The ***Babbie Mason Show*** actually played the song and the YouTube video about my sister who was a drug addict. Some viewers who were struggling with drug addiction actually conveyed how the song ministered to them. One lady called me directly at home a few days after the airing to share how the song ministered to both her and her husband, who struggled with drugs. During a radio interview in Roanoke, Virginia, a listener called in and requested a copy of the same song and shared how special the song was to her. The radio host told the lady if she could come by the station within the next few minutes she would be able to personally meet and chat with me. The lady came by the station with a little girl three or four years old. My husband held the little girl's hand as I ministered to the crying grandmother. She pointed to the little girl and told me: "**Your song is special to me because her daddy is on drugs and I know exactly what your song is talking about. I want my son to hear your song.**" I proudly presented her a copy of my CD for the glory of God. I told her, "*I don't proclaim to be a great singer, but I knew I obeyed God to compose the song.*" I continued, "*If this song was written to minister to no one but you and your son, then my labor was not in vain.*" To me, that is seasoned ministry.

The social media phenomenon has allowed an overwhelming abundance of love toward my family and me. People have ministered to us from near and far. Although I would love to share the names of all the people who have touched my life, I know I cannot without omitting someone. There are a host of people who could have been included in this chapter because so many have been so kind. Many names were thought of, but only a few were chosen *at this time*. But all is not lost; maybe God will allow me to write another book which can possibly include your name! It gives me great honor to include a few honorable mentions in this chapter. By the power vested in me, I do declare and decree blessings over the lives of the people who have contributed to my life through words and deeds.

I offer thanks and honor to **Mrs. Betty Jo Dease** of the **Plantersville Community of Georgetown, South Carolina.** She is not my mother, nor is she my sister, but she served in both capacities during my recuperation from my near-death accident. Betty is a cooking enthusiast who purchased, cooked, and delivered hot meals for my family. I offered several times to reimburse her, but she said, *"No."* I even tried to slip money to her, to no avail—she returned the money! She said, *"No, Ev! I am doing this from my heart because I love you and your family."* Betty Jo, surprisingly, cooked my entire Thanksgiving dinner in 2014. There was not even a need to use the microwave oven this day! Even though I am able to move about independently, Betty continues to check on me and offer her assistance. Betty Jo has shown me what it really *looks* like to serve my fellowman. Oh, I forgot to mention: Betty Jo prepared my complete Mother's Day dinner May 10, 2015. She conspired with my husband and my boys over the telephone to cunningly deliver **my empty pots over to her house before I returned home.** They gave her the worst pots in the house, my favorite ones they so often see me use. Betty returned the old pots full of my favorite treats. I enjoyed the meal, but was disappointed that my men did not take my new set of stainless cookware to Betty Jo's house. My husband said, *"Maybe you'll get rid of those old ugly pots now, I betcha!"* We all laughed about it later! I was blessed on Sunday, May 31, 2015 to publicly recognize Betty Jo after my speaking engagement and offer appreciation for all the love and support she has rendered to my family. And, yes, I am still using my old ugly pots!

    A faithful friend, **Evangelist Cynthia Myers** of the **Plantersville Community, Georgetown, South Carolina,** is such a blessing in my life as she calls my name to our Heavenly Father in prayer. I am forever grateful because she could be utilizing her time to do other things, but she sacrifices on my behalf. There is an Adopt-A-Highway sign in the community that bears my name where Sister Cynthia was led by Holy Spirit to pray for my recovery from the accident. Many drove past the sign as she prayed, but they didn't all understand; still, she interceded on my behalf. She told me that prayer-request letters for my recovery were distributed throughout the community. Oh, what a blessing! It is such an honor to have been thought of in such a unique way. More so, it is a blessing to know that such an anointed vessel is bombarding Heaven for me. Thank you, Sister Cynthia, for serving me as King Saul's son, Jonathan, provided services to the elect-king David.

I received this text message below from another one of my dear sisters in Christ on August 14, 2014. I looked at the date (8, 14, and 14) and what a double blessing I received from her ministering to me as Holy Spirit led her. This was an unexpected blessing indeed:

> *This is what the Lord gave me for you. The title is Beauty…beauty for your Ashes. The pain of the old lump had to be removed for me to restore you so that my new oil could be poured into you. An equal balance and a just weight is what I require of you. A flower blossom; but, in order for it to rise anew, it must die to regenerate its new body, leaves, petals and to bring a fresh and glorious color of its life. Beauty for your ashes—what a beautiful flower you are! I shall rebuild your temple for My Spirit resides in you. For you must rise for my glory…Beauty (Psalm 48 and Isaiah 61).*

Sister Lenore Brunson
Bronx, New York (formerly of Manning, South Carolina)

> *To all of my friends and families: I am asking all of you to please pray for my friend and your friend and sister in Christ, Evelyn Murray Drayton. She was in a really bad car accident on Sunday. Keep her*

and her family in prayer and very close to your heart. God is a good GOD and He hears all our prayers. Thank you.
Roberta Mention
Hemingway, South Carolina

GOD bless you all for your many prayers and support during this journey for my Auntie Evelyn! She's progressing and healing day by day! She looks great physically—and spiritually, she is certainly a child of GOD. GOD has His hands on her and she's recovering unbelievably! She's still encouraging and ministering to others as she has always before the accident! She's humble through all of this and still praising GOD! She is very faithful, strong, and most definitely resilient! Please keep your prayers coming! Thank you all and God bless. Love, the Drayton/Murray family!

Diane Conyers (my niece)
Manning, South Carolina

No longer on my birthday do I look for materialistic gifts, but I look for blessings and favor. I just want to thank God for sparing my life and blessing me to be alive and to see another birthday. Thank you all for the love and birthday messages, texts, posts, and phone calls...I love you all to life. But the greatest blessing I received today on my birthday is to see Evangelist Evelyn Murray Drayton post on Facebook today for the first time since her accident. Please read her testimony below. God is real and still working miracles...

"DADDY," our Heavenly Father, has blessed me in

ways that I don't know adequate words to describe. (Bleeding on the brain, head wound, broken back, broken ribs, broken leg, damaged lungs, and pneumonia---to name a few...all at the same time) and here I am on FB to say thanks for all prayers, phone calls, cards, messages, hospital visits—THANK YOU!! I will be headed to my own house soon (leaving rehab in a few days). I am one grateful daughter and my life will never be the same. Let no one entice you to turn your back on God. His Son Jesus Christ is still the ANSWER! Love you all. Evelyn

Jonathan Grant (Cooper)
Georgetown, South Carolina, *United States Marine*

Evelyn, you healed so fast it didn't seem to make sense because I witnessed how your body was broken. It's almost unbelievable. I love you, Baby Sister.

Dorothy Murray (my biological sister)
Manning, South Carolina

What can I say? If God is with you, who can be against you? Not even the devil and all of his

demons in hell can take your life and make you quit God. Continue to be strong in the Lord and trust God for where He wants to take you. The thief comes but to kill, steal and destroy. The Lord protected you and said to Satan, "Not yet." The sincere prayer of a righteous person, in the name of Jesus, will heal the sick. I have faith to believe you will recover. The words that you posted are like a mirror in my soul. I will continue, with the help of the Holy Spirit, to be guided by them. Thank you for the uplift, Dr. Evelyn Murray Drayton!

Reverend Dr. Richard A. Brown
Georgetown, South Carolina

Evelyn, you are the best! I enjoyed our conversation so much. The light (beacon) that God has bestowed upon you is for YOU. I thank GOD for using you as His vessel to encourage women from all walks of life. Stay encouraged and surrounded with like-minded people who acknowledge your light! True clarity and humbleness are what women of ALL ages and walks of life need now; so, I am looking forward to YOUR conference/symposium. While a conference I know will touch many hearts, your calling and charge on your life is much greater than a planned conference. God's calling on your life is so POWERFUL! Again, stay encouraged and stay with like-minded people for God always gets the GLORY. Keep me posted BECAUSE GOD IS CALLING. God's blessing on your ministry always. Love you, my Sister.

Shelia Grier
Charleston, South Carolina (formerly of Georgetown, South Carolina)

Rise up, Sister Drayton, there is even greater works for you to do Mighty Woman of God. You shall recover and be healed in Jesus' Name! I am continuing always praying for you and that God will continue to bless you and prosper you in every area of your life. Thank you also for being a blessing to me and supporting me in my business endeavors and being a prayer warrior on my behalf. I appreciate you so much. God bless you in your book writing. You have a precious and wise gift that God has anointed you with. Love you and God bless you, Sister Drayton!

Harriett Bromell
Georgetown, South Carolina

Sister Wilma Warren inspired me to include the word "***possible***" in my book title based on her message below and our other communications.

Dr. Evelyn, I love you and I thank God for your speedy recovery. Here is one wink, one thumbs up, and one in Jesus' name full recovery. I know God is able to work miracles....You are a MIRACLE. I shall not stop praying. I shall not stop believing God. He is faithful and He is able. I love you. I am praying for you. God is awesomely wonderful. In my sleep I saw your name spelled CORRECTLY. He did not speak—just showed your name. Several times I tried to wake up, but He would not let me open my eyes until He showed me your FULL name. He is saying that there is a gift of healing on your life and He is beginning to use it for His glory and for your good. There is more—He said while you were in the coma you received the GIFT OF HEALING... then He allowed me to open my eyes...God bless you. While you were in the coma you were 100 percent in His presence... Glory! God favors me and trusts me with His power. Oh, my God. I bless the Lord this day for his grace and mercy. "POSSIBLE!" You represent what is POSSIBLE with God. I'm smiling. Thank you for praying from afar for Jimmy's supernatural healing. That, too, was in my sleep. God said, "You" all the way across town... now watch HIM work through you. Chills! Thank you so much...Thank you and the rest will become a part of history...it is a done deal by faith. AMEN. Done by faith! I thank God for you, Dr. Evelyn....MIRACLE that you are...and my inspiration to PRESS! I love you and I thank God for your speedy recovery. I SHALL NOT stop believing God. He is Faithful and He is able.

Wilma Warren
St. Louis, Missouri

My Sister, I'm praying for you always. God is on your side and you are coming out of this with new visions and ministries. God works with the broken. After all that you have been through, it will be nothing in comparison to where GOD is taking you. Your latter days WILL be your greatest! Listen and hear what GOD is saying to you, write the VISION. Love you my Sister, <u>NOW FAITH MINISTRIES with Evangelist Arlene E. Henry</u>

Evangelist Arlene Henry
Woodbridge, Connecticut

Evangelist Arlene Henry sent me a question on Saturday February 21, 2015, asking if I am familiar with the words, **"A Place Where Time Stops."** I had never heard of those words together in a book, song, poem, or anything. Later, I searched the words and found they were quite popular on the Internet. I pondered the words and related them to the time in my life when it really seemed like time had stopped—that is the time after I had the accident. Due to the medically induced coma, I do not recall weeks of my life that just passed me by. I don't even recall the accident. So I can relate to those words that were dropped in her spirit.

> *YOU ARE A WALKING TESTIMONY of the goodness of our Lord, Jesus! It's so good to read your progress report "in part" because I know there was a lot of exercising faith, confessing faith, confessing the word, overcoming the enemy, combating the flesh, and a lot more in dealing with your progressive recovery. Just keep doing what you're doing and you know our God is faithful to His word. Hallelujah!*

Myra Robinson
Florence, South Carolina

> *You shall overcome all obstacles victoriously and triumphantly simply because of who your Father, judge, master and savior is. Weeping may endure for a night but joy shall come in the morning. God did not bring you this far to leave you. He only gave you a more intensifying testimony to share with others. Keep your head up. I pray for you and you pray for me. God has not forgotten.*

DW, a good friend
Charlotte, North Carolina

Sister Evelyn, Hope this note finds you in perfect peace and that you are encouraged to know that 2015 is going to be our Breakout year. Love you and appreciate your prayers. (Sister Kellie and I have never met face to face; we've only seen each other's photos and communicate only by U.S. mail and telephone. Yet this woman has been such a blessing in my life. I attended my first Benny Hinn crusade at her expense. God has truly blessed her to be a blessing in my life.)

Kellie Copeland Burnup
Ridgeville, South Carolina

Dr. Evelyn Murray Drayton, I thank God for your words of encouragement and prayer. You have now empowered me to walk stronger in my faith. You're another witness from the Lord. I see that you're a mighty soldier on the battlefield. As you are healing, just think about other lives you are touching or have touched—glory to God. He is awesome! I'll always keep you and your family lifted in prayer.

Ben Sessions
Florence, South Carolina

What a testimony! I thank God for my sister and how God is rapidly healing her body from the inside out. God spared your life, Sister, because there is much more work for you to do.

Fenia Ragin
Summerton, South Carolina

I had the privilege of hearing Evelyn Drayton's awesome testimony at church last night! She is the picture of health. I met her husband and learned that he also is an overcomer [cancer]. Evelyn is grateful for this prayer group and many others, for she was lifted up in prayer while she was unable to pray for herself. She mentioned **Mary Canteen** *numerous times during her testimony. It was obvious that Mary has been a huge blessing to Evelyn and her family. Please be reminded, prayer warriors, prayer really does work. "Casting all your care upon Him; for He careth for you" (I Peter 5:7).*

Barbara S. Pratt
Moncks Corner, South Carolina

My God, woman of God! It was good seeing you on Saturday at the **Preach the Word Worldwide Television Network** *on-location taping in Florence, South Carolina. Not only are you walking, you are preaching the word with power and authority! God has truly given you the ability to walk in the natural and to walk in the spirit as well. Wow! What an awesome God we serve! If you had not told me that you had been in such a major accident, I would not have known it by looking at you! Not a scar that I could see...only your lovely radiance as usual! I am in total agreement with your "Thank you, JESUS!" Hope to see you again soon. Peace and Blessings! Love you much!*

Pearline Fryson
Tallahassee, Florida

Couldn't let the day end without telling you Happy Mother's Day 2015! You are an excellent mother and role model to other mothers everywhere. Hope you enjoyed your day. God bless.

Veronica "Vonnie" Drayton Coles, Charlotte, North Carolina (formerly of Georgetown, South Carolina)

Each of us has a testimony about something that we experienced in life, whether or not it is pertaining to survival, recovery, healing, or grieving. Each of us can probably attest that someone offered us words of encouragement or some form of support during those challenging times. My medical care was intense and I will never be able to fully express my thanks to everyone who contributed to my overall well-being. I thank all of the first responders and the staff at McLeod who were vital in nursing me back to health. As a matter of fact, I was so spoiled with loving care that I almost did not want to sever ties from McLeod's trauma unit. I am grateful for all the different medical facilities and staff, the occupational and physical therapists, and the speech pathologists—just to name a few, that cared for me and assisted with my recovery. All of the facilities, for the most part, were exceptional.

 I am also appreciative for the support from family and friends. I thank God for those who offered words of encouragement and prepared full-course meals for my family. Friends even provided clothes that were suitable for lounging around the house and for dressy events. I also thank God for the many individuals that visited, telephoned, sent get-well cards, sent flowers, and or offered prayers. Those of you who tucked in monetary gifts know that God will reward your cheerful giving. Your support made a difference in my fight for life. My healing is an inspiration to my entire community. I pray that we, as a community, continue to stand together collectively to bring about positive transformation among those we cross paths with from day to day, whether in sickness or in health. Ladies and gentlemen, I truly thank God for all of your encouraging words and for being the vessels through which the words were delivered. I believe I have witnessed the growth of your confidence in my Kingdom identity and to all of you, I say, *"Thank you!"*

Last, but not least, my husband and my two sons gave me extraordinary loving care. I am resigned to the inevitability that we all will die someday, but my husband did not withhold or withdraw any treatment that would have led to my gradual and eventual death. I thank God for my husband who consented for the medical staff to use various methods to help conserve and sustain my life. Everything I needed was provided. My husband even cared for my personal, medical, and hygiene needs upon my return home.

We must be determined to overcome and offer thanksgiving for each day of life and for those who are a part of our lives. When we have a heart for people, we may have to open our lips and encourage someone else while we live—just as my relatives and friends did for me. There were times Jesus cried out in a loud voice and there were times He whispered in a still small voice. "What I tell you in the dark, speak in the daylight; what is whispered in your ear, proclaim from the roofs" (Matthew 10:27 NIV). Then there are times we are to be quiet—time to be totally silent! I have concluded that there are times we must speak loud and spare not. I cry loudly now to say, ***Thank you!***

"And I will bless them that bless thee"
(Genesis 12:3)

What is the Lord speaking to your heart today? Are you ready to go and bless someone?

"My sheep hear my voice, and I know them, and they follow me: And I give unto them eternal life; and they shall never perish, neither shall any man pluck them out of my hand" (John 10:27-28).

"I will hear what God the LORD will speak: for he will speak peace unto his people, and to his saints: but let them not turn again to folly" (Psalm 85:8).

"And the LORD came, and stood, and called as at other times, Samuel, Samuel. Then Samuel answered, Speak; for thy servant heareth" (I Samuel 3:10).

"Thou shalt also decree a thing, and it shall be established unto thee: and the light shall shine upon thy ways" (Job 22:28).

"Death and life are in the power of the tongue: and they that love it shall eat the fruit thereof" (Proverbs 18:21).

"Therefore whosoever heareth these sayings of mine, and doeth them, I will liken him unto a wise man, which built his house upon a rock" (Matthew 7:24).

SPEAK LORD

Chapter Five
Endless Possibilities

"But Jesus beheld them, and said unto them, 'With men this is impossible; but with God all things are possible'" (Matthew 19:26).

With such a profusion of knowledge available to us today, we are witnessing some amazing things in this world. Some are seen and some are unseen. There is not a logical explanation for all of these occurrences. Peace and tranquility most certainly sound good during these trying and testing times in which we live. These are highly sought-after states of mind, knowing that life offers many unexpected possibilities. Some days of possibilities are like breaths of fresh air and rays of sunshine, while many others are full of gloom and doom. No one knows what a day may bring, but just being alive to experience the possibilities is a blessing. Proverbs 27:1 reminds us of our limitation when compared to God's unlimited knowledge of each day's events. He has endless facts about life for which we only make assumptions.

Each of us experience challenges on a daily basis. We encounter these differing experiences for various reasons unique to our earthly assignments. Some people believe that the reason they went through a time of testing should also be the same reason for your testing. This is not a valid assumption indicative of our uniqueness and our purpose.

Our chief purpose is to honor and glorify God! Even though we hear about tragedies on a daily basis, we must still trust God. We are to trust that whatever God allows—even trouble—will ultimately work together for our good. Our dynamic and engaging faith in our caring God will stabilize our footing and fortify our confidence in His ability to mightily use our gifts for His glory. Even through crisis, Father God has equipped, strengthened and enabled us for His greater purpose. His Power will be gloriously manifested in and through our lives. We must thank the Lord Jesus that He will give us clarity for the greater vision for our lives through His word, the Bible. God will anoint our divine calling and bestow wisdom beyond measure upon our lives to accomplish His Mighty plans perfectly, completely, and obediently.

When difficult and challenging situations arise, we have a tendency to worry rather than trust God, who specializes in the impossible. Although life is fragile and uncertain, we are encouraged and assured in Matthew 19:26 that *"with God all things are possible."* If something is possible, it means that thing can be done or achieved. The key to possibilities is one's belief in the word of God. Jesus said unto him, *"If thou canst believe, all things are possible to him that believeth"* (Mark 9:23). Because we believe, there is nothing that we propose to achieve that cannot be done. Once we decide what we want to achieve, we can attain it because Christ is our strength. Dream big and achieve big!

Tomorrow is not promised to any of us. We must take time to enjoy the unique moments in life that we can often take for granted. With that being said, we must take time to love and live. Life is truly a gift; and other blessings belong to us for enjoyment each day that God blesses us on this earth. James 4:14 reminds us that life is compared to a vapor that lasts for only a moment and then vanishes. Blessings have been known to overtake people and people have been known to miss blessings. It seems that just before receiving blessings there is often some type of antagonistic encounter, whether it is by someone or something, orchestrated to distract us from pursuing our blessings. Frankly, sometimes at the brink of a blessing we have to brace ourselves for backlashes—even suffering. We can become so bombarded with various distractions that time can pass us by without us garnering a fraction of what we could have learned, earned, or even discerned.

Things happen in our lives to force us to make choices. Some people handle surprises well, even tragedies, but others succumb. Each of us must give an account for how we confront and handle our challenges. We cannot merely imitate others and think their way is the best way for our situation. Are you trying to walk in someone else's shoes to attain your blessings? **Be yourself!** Your own shoes will fit perfectly when they are designed specifically for you. Even though your shoes are tight momentarily, just walk in your shoes for a little while and your feet will feel better. Do your feet still hurt? Well, don't try to walk in another person's shoes and expect them to fit perfectly. In the same way, God wants you to walk the path that has been designed for your life. Again, **be yourself!** God has laid out His plan specifically for you and your assignment will not work for anybody else, only you. We don't have to duplicate or imitate the action of another, we only have to be ourselves and do the things that can bring love, laughter, and life to another sister or a brother. Don't get trapped in someone else's dogma! Trying to imitate another person's life is not the way God will have you go.

Walk in your own shoes—make your own path—and God will make that path straight for you. We must walk the path that leads us in the right direction. Sometimes, though, we can interrupt our walk by remaining in one place too long. We cannot remain in a place that does not bear fruit in our lives. We need to be strong and not lean on someone or something that may prevent us from bearing fruit. We can become so comfortable and lackadaisical that we yearn for complacency in all the wrong places. The same way David would have suffered defeat if armed for battle wearing Saul's military equipment, imitating another's life path will, likewise, result in your defeat. David knew where His help came from and had no fear. Jesus is the only person we should totally lean on to help us walk the path of life. This path offers and leads us to a prepared place, if only we are willing to take the arduous expedition. Take the journey and always be steadfast and strong in the Lord for your survival.

- Do an assessment of your life. Are things going well? Are things really looking good for you right now? Great! Congratulations!
- Be confident that everything negative that happens to you is NOT punishment for something you have said or done. It could be an attack of the enemy for your distraction and, ultimately, your destruction.

A magnetic name tag *Evelyn* was displayed on a store rack, indicating that *Evelyn* means *"new life."* How did my mother know to name me *Evelyn* and that God would give me a second chance at life? I say *second* chance, but I know I've already had more than two opportunities to live! My mother probably didn't know the full meaning of my name, but God most certainly did! There are times we may be tempted to embellish the truth about ourselves, but God already knows us. I can write a sermon using Psalm 103:14-15 and title it **Who Do You Think You Are?** *"For he knoweth our frame; he remembereth that we are dust. As for man, his days are as grass: as a flower of the field, so he flourisheth. For the wind passeth over it, and it is gone; and the place thereof shall know it no more."* That passage of Scripture definitely reminds me of my frailty.

My smile widens to think about how my name correlates to my *"new life"* in Christ and my second chance at life on this earth. We were in God's mind before the creation of the world, which means our coming into the world was predetermined before our parents met. My mother had prophesied my destiny of *new life* by naming me

Evelyn. If my mother were alive today, I could only surmise that she would be proud to read her baby girl's story about the ways God has manifested Himself in her life. I had to be born again, though! My life took on new meaning many years ago when I accepted Jesus Christ as my Lord and Savior. I am now a child of the King of this universe. I stumbled and fell along the way since that initial decision, but thank God He kept picking me up as a good Father would. I am everything God says I am. These scriptures helped me and I believe they will help you also:

- He *knows us by name* and *will be with us* (Isaiah 43:1-2).
- He has *a plan* for our lives (Jeremiah 29:11).
- He has our names engraved *on the palms of His hands* (Isaiah 49:16); and
- He *will not forget* us (Isaiah 49:15).

For those reasons, in all honesty, I can no longer allow other people's opinions to dictate what I write or how I live my life as a follower of Christ. Unlike a narcissist, I believe I am a fun-loving individual with gregarious laughter, who loves nurturing and sharing the Good News of Jesus Christ. God gave me abundant life and a purpose upon believing and accepting Jesus into my life. I believe His Son Jesus, the Christ, was born, died, was buried, and resurrected. Hence, I have abdicated my role of trying to be god over my life. My testimonial mantra is forever *"Jesus, Jesus, Jesus."* I am learning to allow God to use me in any way He desires in order to facilitate His plan (I Corinthians 8:6). I am honored to be alive to share the wonders of God. He has given me another chance to live life to the fullest. I became a joint heir with Christ when I believed in Jesus Christ and received Him as a gift given to us by God, our Heavenly Father. God has equipped and assigned me as a **"*possibility expert*"** and this is my way of glorifying my Father. This role helps me to attest that faith without works is dead. My goal is to use my messages, writings, and music to help others spiritually, emotionally, physically, and mentally. I am here to help others overcome challenges in life—helping them reach their fullest potential and pursue unlimited possibilities. Unlike church pastors, I do not have a specific audience to minister to, so my speaking, books, and music are my ministry tools. My products are not for career advancement, but are for a platform to be a more effective witness. It is common knowledge that I cannot reach all, but I can reach some!

Being part of the 21st-century generation is not an accident. The world needs us because there is something in us that only we have to offer this age group. Someone may ask me, *"What are you doing?"* My response possibly will be, *"I am busy bearing the infirmities* [weaknesses or failings] *of my sisters and brothers; and I hope you are doing the same for me."* Even though that response sounds farfetched, that is exactly what Romans 15:1 tells us that we *"ought to do."* Contrarily, we are turning aside and living for ourselves and no one else. I am finding out that we have not lived until we have shared a part of us with someone else. The whole creation is groaning for our manifestation as a child of God. We can rise to fulfill our divine assignment. We must rise and shine, for our light has come and the glory of God is risen upon us (Isaiah 60:1). Even if no one tells us, we must know that kings and princes are coming to the brightness of our rising. Although I have been a thoughtful and engaging mentor to many young people over the years, many people are waiting for our light to shine so that they are redeemed to our Heavenly Father. Many will hear of us very soon. We will not fail this generation to help them follow Jesus Christ.

My foundation in life is Jesus (I Corinthians 3:11) and I want to be as sincere and structured as was the early church. They suffered, and many died, to ensure that the message of Jesus and the cross live on. The Book of Isaiah sheds light on who Jesus really is and highlights the spiritual gifts He has shared with us:

> *"And the spirit of the* LORD *shall rest upon him, the spirit of wisdom and understanding, the spirit of counsel and might, the spirit of knowledge and of the fear of the* LORD; *And shall make him of quick understanding in the fear of the* LORD: *and he shall not judge after the sight of his eyes, neither reprove after the hearing of his ears: But with righteousness shall he judge the poor, and reprove with equity for the meek of the earth: and he shall smite the earth: with the rod of his mouth, and with the breath of his lips shall he slay the wicked. And righteousness shall be the girdle of his loins, and faithfulness the girdle of his reins"* (Isaiah 11:2-5).

Now it is easy to say, *"But that was Jesus."* Well, let's look at some others given the spirit of wisdom:

> *"And Joshua the son of Nun was full of the spirit of wisdom; for Moses had laid his hands upon him"* (Deuteronomy 34:9)

> *"And delivered him [Joseph] out of all his afflictions, and gave him favour and wisdom in the sight of Pharaoh, king of Egypt; and he made him governor over Egypt and all his house"* (Acts 7:10).

> *"That the God of our Lord Jesus Christ, the Father of glory, may give unto you true believers the spirit of wisdom and revelation in the knowledge of him"* (Ephesians 1:17).

God's word is wisdom and it brings cleansing to our life. It is God who speaks to us and distributes gifts and graces to do His will. Discovering your purpose in God's Kingdom is awesome. I follow Christ, but it is interesting to study some other great biblical characters:

- Be like David and Joshua, who were patient and courageous
- Be like Esther, who was willing to perish for her obedience to go before the king
- Be like Joseph, who left the pit and operated in his continual season of grace and favor
- Be like Job, who received double for his trouble
- Be yourself and be prepared to reap what you have sown

There comes a time we must stand on the biblical truth that we sometimes take for granted or merely quote in times of catastrophe. Disastrous experiences are targeted not only to silence our voices but to literally destroy our lives as we search for truth. Like a vast number of people, we have faced many challenges in life and were sustained with much prayer and praise. It may be difficult to *"count it all joy"* (James 1:2) when negative things happen to positive people; but things will happen to us at some point in our life. Brent Barnett sums it so well when he asserts:

> *I know from personal experience as do you that we all suffer at one time or another and in various ways. Not only do we suffer personally, but we suffer as we watch those whom we love endure pain. Sometimes God intervenes and removes suffering miraculously and supernaturally. Yet many times, He does not. Of course, God has purposes in suffering, using it to build up our character, develop in us perseverance, and purify our hearts and motives as we learn that He is all that we ever needed and that He can be trusted even during the storm, whether He calms it or not. Christ suffered deeply. All of the apostles were severely persecuted, and eleven out of twelve were brutally executed.*

Suffering is a reality, yet strangely we do not understand it well, let alone handle it properly.
Thank You for Suffering So That I Don't Have To
http://www.relevantbibleteaching.com by Brent Barnett

With those strong words from Brent Barnett, we can feel comfortable singing in unison, "**I am stronger now because of all the things I have been through.**" Some of us could have possibly been voted to be the person least likely to survive the seemingly impossible things that we have encountered. But we did it anyway! My vehicle was involved in a horrific head-on collision and landed me on life support, but I thank God I am still alive to write my intriguing story. Some may ascertain my story to be nonsensical as I share the madness, paranoia, and forgetfulness while I was weaned from the ventilator. Through it all, I was favored and honored to share the personal cataclysmic event of my life.

"The thief cometh not, but for to steal, and to kill, and to destroy: I am come that they might have life, and that they might have it more abundantly" (John 10:10).

"Be sober, be vigilant; because your adversary the devil, as a roaring lion, walketh about, seeking whom he may devour" (I Peter 5:8).

"I shall not die, but live, and declare the works of the Lord" (Psalm 118:17).

"Before I was afflicted I went astray, but now I obey your word" (Psalm 119:67 NIV)

"I know, LORD, that your laws are righteous, and that in faithfulness you have afflicted me" (Psalm 119:75 NIV).

"Lord, by such things people live; and my spirit finds life in them too. You restored me to health and let me live" (Isaiah 38:16 NIV).

"For he does not willingly bring affliction or grief to anyone" (Lamentations 3:33 NIV).

"Whereas ye know not what shall be on the morrow. For what is your life? It is even a vapour, that appeareth for a little time, and then vanisheth away" (James 4:14).

"Boast not thyself of tomorrow; for thou knowest not what a day may bring forth" (Proverbs 27:1).

Chapter Six

A Recipe for Healing

"Is any sick among you? let him call for the elders of the church; and let them pray over him, anointing him with oil in the name of the Lord" (James 5:14).

Healing is a gift to the Body of Christ. It is my desire to spread awareness of God's healing power. I want my journey to be seen and used by others as a positive learning experience. There are things we see in life, but we have no earthly idea how to explain them. We are sometimes surprised when God heals a person who appears to be on death's bed. Life is full of such surprises, not to God, but to us. Notice that the words *"health"* and *"healeth"* look closely related. *"For I am the LORD that healeth thee"* (Exodus 15:26).

    First of all, God is not just "a healer," He is **"The Healer."** Many of us are fully able and capable to read the word of God and tell of His goodness. Yet we cannot explain why some people live longer than others or receive no healing at all in this life. We can maintain good health, but we cannot explain why some people heal faster than others. God has given His children authority, but we don't have the last word on healing or any other part of ministry. That is no reason to stop learning or encouraging others to pray for the sick; neither is that a reason not to call on the elders of the church. The things we can explain need to be shared as an inspirational moment for someone else. We can make a difference when we share our wisdom, knowledge, and understanding with others.

Similar to a delicious cooked dish, healing comes with some **necessary** ingredients. Chefs sometime include one extra-special ingredient to a dish and captivate us with a brand-new taste. At the same time, life can be very inclusive, but extra ingredients are meaningless without the basic **right** and **necessary** ingredients. For example, *bread* tastes good, but we won't call it *cake* without *necessary* ingredients. You know—the right amount of sugar, the butter, etc.

Likewise, healing requires *necessary* ingredients—whether the required healing is physical, spiritual, mental, emotional, moral, economic, social, or financial. Ingredients for healing include prayer, confession, repentance, faith, forgiveness, **love, love, love**, trust, compassion, and expectation of answered prayer. Feel free to throw in some other ingredients for a special taste, if you choose. However, with the basic ingredients that I listed, you can expect a change in your life.

A healed body of believers can be of great service to the plan of God. Sure, participating in church services and doing good deeds may be good extra ingredients, but without *salvation*, your results still will not yield God's best for your life.

God has a plan for each of us and, thus, God is still healing and giving assignments to His children. We cannot become weary and give up due to unpleasant situations. There will always be circumstances that challenge our faith, but we must be willing and ready to endure hardness as a good soldier of Jesus Christ. Again, God is not just "a healer," He is "**The Healer.**" Claim your healing! Trust God, stay strong in faith, and stay focused.

> (*This message of encouragement has been disseminated in print to a number of people prior to completing this book. Copyrighted © January 8, 2015*).

I admire my friend, **Barbara S. Pratt** of Moncks Corner, South Carolina, for obeying the prompting of Holy Spirit to share the word of God with so many of His children who are dealing with various sicknesses—many who have been diagnosed with cancer. My husband, Russell, like Barbara, is also a cancer survivor! She mailed a Healing Scripture packet to him and sent a courtesy packet for me as well. While Barbara's packet contains a plethora of scriptures, I have chosen only a few of the inspiring verses from the King James Version (KJV) to encourage you and inspire resilience—and to draw others into God's Kingdom.

> *"And said, If thou wilt diligently hearken to the voice of the* LORD *thy God, and wilt do that which is right in his sight, and wilt give ear to his commandments, and keep all his statutes, I will put none of these diseases upon thee, which I have brought upon the Egyptians: for I am the* LORD *that healeth thee"* (Exodus 15:26).

> *"And the Lord will take away from thee all sickness, and will put none of the evil diseases of Egypt, which thou knowest, upon thee; but will lay them upon all them that hate thee"* (Deuteronomy 7:15).

> *"Turn again, and tell Hezekiah the captain of my people, Thus saith the Lord, the God of David thy father, I have heard thy prayer, I have seen thy tears: behold, I will heal thee: on the third day thou shalt go up unto the house of the Lord"* (2 Kings 20:5).

> *"The Lord will strengthen him upon the bed of languishing: thou wilt make his bed in his sickness"* (Psalms 41:3).

"Bless the Lord, O my soul, and forget not all his benefits: Who forgiveth all thine iniquities; who healeth all thy diseases; Who redeemeth thy life from destruction; who crowneth thee with lovingkindness and tender mercies; Who satisfieth thy mouth with good things; so that thy youth is renewed like the eagle's" (Psalm 103:2-5).

"He sent his word, and healed them, and delivered them from their destructions" (Psalm 107:20).

"Pleasant words are as an honeycomb, sweet to the soul, and health to the bones" (Proverbs 16:24).

"A merry heart doeth good like a medicine: but a broken spirit drieth the bones" (Proverbs 17:22).

"But they that wait upon the LORD shall renew their strength; they shall mount up with wings as eagles; they shall run, and not be weary; and they shall walk, and not faint" (Isaiah 40:31).

"Fear thou not; for I am with thee: be not dismayed; for I am thy God: I will strengthen thee; yea, I will help thee; yea, I will uphold thee with the right hand of my righteousness" (Isaiah 41:10).

"But he was wounded for our transgressions, he was bruised for our iniquities: the chastisement of our peace was upon him; and with his stripes we are healed" (Isaiah 53:5).

"No weapon that is formed against thee shall prosper; and every tongue that shall rise against thee in judgment thou shalt condemn. This is the heritage of the servants of the LORD, and their righteousness is of me, saith the LORD" (Isaiah 54:17).

"Heal me, O LORD, and I shall be healed; save me, and I shall be saved: for thou art my praise" (Jeremiah 17:14).

"For I will restore health unto thee, and I will heal thee of thy wounds, saith the LORD; because they called thee an Outcast, saying, This is Zion, whom no man seeketh after" (Jeremiah 30:17).

"Behold, I will bring it health and cure, and I will cure them, and will reveal unto them the abundance of peace and truth" (Jeremiah 33:6).

"And Jesus went about all Galilee, teaching in their synagogues, and preaching the gospel of the kingdom, and healing all manner of sickness and all manner of disease among the people" (Matthew 4:23).

"Is any sick among you? Let him call for the elders of the church; and let them pray over him, anointing him with oil in the name of the Lord: And the prayer of faith shall save the sick, and the Lord shall raise him up; and if he have committed sins, they shall be forgiven him. Confess your faults one to another, and pray one for another, that ye may be healed. The effectual fervent prayer of a righteous man availeth much" (James 5:14-16).

"Beloved, I wish above all things that thou mayest prosper and be in health, even as thy soul prospereth" (3 John 1:2).

"When Jesus heard that, he said, This sickness is not unto death, but for the glory of God, that the Son of God might be glorified thereby" (John 4:11).

I have never been bedridden due to sickness, other than for childbearing reasons and the motor vehicle accident. I have never been the primary caretaker to the ill;

nonetheless, I have surrounded the sick with visitation and prayers over the years. It was not unusual to hear smart, well-meaning people say, "If I were you, I would take this medicine" or "If I were you, I would do this." Advice is plenteous since it is free and can be offered by anyone—even if bad advice is given. Yet, when a sick person is being cared for, it takes more than advice. It also takes a willing worker and a helping hand—and trust me—sharing the word of God can also bring comfort to those who accept it.

Convalescents can possibly become frustrated if they feel neglected or unloved due to constant demands or reliance on their primary caregivers, especially if the caregivers are family members. At the same time, family members can become frustrated and burnt-out by the negative or unappreciative attitude of the invalids in their care. One thing that seems to resonate with me, though, is that one arrogant family member of a sick person can lead a caretaker to believe whatever services provided to the patient are never good enough! The same egotistical family member can hinder an entire community from offering viable support to a sick loved one who is in dire need of assistance.

The sick can sometimes compare the seemingly momentary special attention received from nonfamily members to that of his or her daily caregivers. It can be overwhelming for the caregivers to correct the sick person's abusive or negative messages whispered or portrayed of them to outsiders or occasional visitors. The verbal abuse emitted from patients can possibly result in maltreatment by the caregivers, if left unmonitored. When a caregiver is sick, he or she may still struggle to care for another sick person. Even the best workers can become ill or feel discouraged when providing their very best services and afterward have the recipients constantly belittle them in the public eye. This can turn into an outright argument if things are not handled properly and in a timely manner. No matter the situation, a sick person needs tender, loving care. Should you ever find yourself on a sick list, here are some additional

suggestions (or should I dare say advice) you may want to consider:

Healing Tips I Learned Over the Years
1. Visit your doctor and obey your doctor's orders. If the doctor tells you to avoid specific foods or drinks, please heed the warnings.
2. Take medication only as prescribed by your doctor. If your instructions say ONLY AS NEEDED then obey—especially for painkillers. Doctors know how to select the best medication regiment for your specific bodily condition. We take their advice in good faith, knowing there are rare cases where some patients have been misdiagnosed or dispensed the wrong medication. To take or not to take medication is still your choice, but obedience is important for a speedy recovery.
3. Talk with your doctor and don't be ashamed or afraid to express your concerns.
4. Do what you can to help yourself. For example, if you are asked to raise your arm, even if you don't feel like it, do it anyway. It is for your benefit, not the doctor's or the caregiver's benefit.
5. Move your body, when possible, to stay active. Don't just sit, eat, and sleep. Move your body parts!
6. Don't overwork your body or overdose on medication thinking you will heal faster that way. This negligence can cause a relapse and endanger your life.
7. Avoid negative words like *can't* or *never*. You always have the option to *try and succeed*. Keep your mind thinking on good and pleasant things.
8. Love and appreciate those who are taking time to care for you. Watch your mouth and don't belittle those who sacrifice their lifestyle to accommodate yours.

9. We all love attention, but do NOT manipulate visitors or caregivers to make them believe that you are sicker than you really are to gain their sympathy.
10. Life or death is spoken with the same tongue. Speak life over yourself. Be aware that well-meaning people may come your way speaking negative words or unpleasant words. You must choose to accept or reject words spoken over your life. Just because another person didn't get healed does not mean you cannot be healed!
11. Remember: Luke was a physician, but many people around him remained sick. Jesus, our GREAT PHYSICIAN, walked this earth and implied that many in his hometown were not healed because of unbelief. Do you believe Jesus is your Healer and that you can be made whole?
12. Trust God for your healing—not man, money, or medicine. It is humbling to know that you NEED someone at some point in your life. Put aside shame and your family name! Accept the help, but trust in God.
13. Stay focused on your purpose to gain full recovery.
14. Use your *mustard seed* faith!
15. Drink lots of **W**ater, **A**ctivate your faith, and remember to **R**elax. (In other words, declare **WAR** for your healing.)
16. Declare and decree healing words over your life in Jesus' precious name.
17. Pray, praise, worship, forgive, and do what is just and right before God. ***Get Well SOONer!***

Conclusion

Some of the extenuating circumstances that we encounter can bitterly challenge our faith. It behooves us, however, to remain vigilant even in the midst of our daily troubles. God is not callous to our desperate situations. Things we experience in this life do not come as a surprise to Him. He knew from the beginning of time about you and everything you face from day to day. He knew that Jesus Christ would die and pay the penalty for our sins. He knew that He would give us power and authority over the works of our enemy, Satan. Yet there are some things God allows in our lives for His purpose and plan that works out for our good. He always has a set day of victory for us—a Day 47. Anything is possible with God—even our victory!

It amazes me that God chose me to encounter the fiery trials He permitted to come my way. I am even more astonished at the pain He allowed me to endure. But, when I think of the pain Jesus endured, I know I am right at home in the Master's plan. Several people told me I am blessed to have no recollection of the auto collision; and that, maybe, if I could refresh my memory, I would beg the Lord to help me forget it all. I am a witness that life does not always end with trauma; recovery is possible.

Amazingly, we can learn from people who hurt us or create havoc in our lives. These different experiences can even teach us to grow and how to love—in spite of. We do not have to seek revenge or feel alone in our suffering. We must be willing to adapt to change that can transpire in our lives. We must be willing to suffer *with* and *for* causes at some point in life. However, we cannot allow stress or anger to slip in and hinder our healing. The mindset has to be changed into something positive. It is ideal to turn negative feelings into thoughts of God and His word. I overcame different strongholds and reaped the benefits of speaking God's word over my body. Believing and trusting God with much prayer, hard work, and determination, I confronted obstacles and accomplished many goals. My situation reminds me of these words from one of my friends, **Apostle Sandra Bromell Gainey (Georgetown, South Carolina)**: "It's **possible** to fall down, but it's not **impossible** to get back up again." Surely, my mind had played lots of tricks on me from time to time—but I got back up!

With much discussion with relatives, I am not oblivious to the fact that there was a lot of uncertainty about my survival among some in the medical arena. In my extreme case, Satan's plot was foiled and I survived. Considering my age and serious bodily injuries the day of the accident, my recovery progress has been unbelievable. The recovery process was grueling and painful, but I survived!

I had retired more than 10 years prior to the accident, so I did not have to worry about returning to a job. Thank God I did not have any young children at home to care for either. My two boys are grown and, therefore, I was able to concentrate fully on my healing process. I cannot imagine what it must feel like to be confronted with being the breadwinner, caretaker, and being the ill person, all at the same time. I pray strength for those who may have such a challenge in life.

Keep in mind that God can use Satan's *barriers* and turn them into your *blessings*. We need to not fear death, care little for the opinion of others, and adhere tenaciously to the course we believe will lead to our healing. I was hard-pressed to remain loyal to who I am and not cater to other people's expectations. With God's help, I focused more on what could be rather than what had happened. Instead of dwelling negatively on our injuries' ramifications, I suggest that we thank God for being alive and offer gratefulness for another day's journey. I am so glad I continued to walk, in spite of mental, emotional, and physical distresses. Today, I can walk, talk, write, drive, and be very independent.

During my recovery from massive trauma, I recall attending a women's conference in Charleston, South Carolina, where I was allowed to talk about my healing journey. Not only did I talk, but during the evening session I was able to rejoice in the Lord with a dance. I was able to dance on the leg that was once broken. As a spiritual caveat, prayer and praise coalesce into a single arena of power. Let us not be concerned about the length of our prayer and praise, or try to impress God with fancy words. Neither are we to be concerned about who is watching us as we worship and praise God. We all can be people of prayer and praise when our hearts are pliable enough to move, whenever the Holy Spirit speaks to us. I celebrated my victory through prayer and praise! That praise and dancing placed me in a position of power.

I managed to refocus and look for a brighter day. I had something to look forward to, and I believe Holy Spirit was teaching me wisdom all along the way. God is faithful to me and His wisdom is to work things together for my good. Wisdom told me to trust God! Though I was afflicted and suffered for a season, my promised joy entered one morning. Doesn't that remind you of how Jesus suffered and is now sitting at the right hand of God the Father? His glorious joy came one day and so did my **Day 47**. *"God is my healer."* Again, I trust God's wisdom. My morning has come and the glorious part about this is the *joy* that I am experiencing on the other side of the weeping and pain. Life is a gift from God. *Life is beautiful!*

God has repositioned me! Allow my testimony to water your life and we can both watch God give the increase. Testimonial writing creates a platform to express my love in a great capacity, without reservation. It serves as an inviting multipurpose tool and is instrumental for inspiration, teaching, education, training, and as an experiential facet. My uphill journey encompasses LOVE,

FORGIVENESS, and HEALING, but I know love is the greatest of the three. My message is not prototypical to the world and I know many people do not readily respond to emotional empathy. However, I believe the more time I spend in God's presence, the more beautiful I am becoming for His glory and purpose.

    I want to share the love of God and encourage others to believe that they can endure hardship. I am not accountable for those who have experienced God's miraculous healing power in their lives and then turned their backs on Him after their recovery. I am indeed grateful to be alive to share **my** powerful testimony of God's divine intervention and His healing power. My life has been transformed through my many bona fide experiences. My hopes and dreams are that my transparent influence impacts your life through my trials and triumphant experiences. I emphatically implore you to allow God to touch your life and cause you to make exponential impact through my intriguing story.

    I have found my purpose for writing. As a result of sharing my testimony, I hope you, too, are encouraged to deal with obstacles and challenges in your life. Rest assured my purpose is not based on anecdotal evidence. Each one of us has a Kingdom purpose. We must strive to do things according to God's Kingdom plan and purpose so that His will is done on earth as it is in Heaven. Let's be reasonable! God deals with us on an individual basis; but, He can also use whomever He pleases to accomplish His purpose. It is evident that I know the healing power of God, our Heavenly Father, and so can you.

    I hope that your life will never be the same as I apply the name of Jesus, apply His Word, and apply His blood over the lives of every reader of this book. I hope that your life has been impacted in a great way by hearing my testimony. Remember, anything's possible! Remember, prophecy is real! Even if no one prophesies this truth to you, you can still have a day of victory—a Day 47. Remain bold and vigilant as you are strengthened and encouraged for your spiritual journey, my friend. Even though timing is of great significance, all things are possible. Living for the Lord is possible. We are to live for Him daily believing every day to be our **Day 47**. Let's dream the impossible dreams and know that God can turn them into the possible. God is able to do the miraculous! God is great and life is beautiful!

"But unto you that fear my name shall the Sun of righteousness arise with healing in his wings; and ye shall go forth, and grow up as calves of the stall" (Malachi 4:2).

"But they that wait upon the LORD shall renew their strength; they shall mount up with wings as eagles; they shall run, and not be weary; and they shall walk, and not faint" (Isaiah 40:31).

"But Jesus beheld them, and said unto them, With men this is impossible; but with God all things are possible" (Matthew 19:26).

Pre-Exam Preparation

Surviving any vehicle accident is a blessing. So, I hope you will agree that to survive a near-fatal head-on collision can be a life-changing event. Every aspect of a person's life could be altered by serious or debilitating injuries. You have just witnessed another testimony of how good our Heavenly Father is to us. I believe you have been blessed as you read my amazing story.

We are now headed to the self-examination room. I believe you will agree that we must be ready at all times because we never know when our last day is on this earth. RIGHT? Let's think about our last complete physical exam. You know the doctors asked questions and examined us very carefully. RIGHT?

We agree that God is good to us. Now, let's search ourselves and see how good we are to our Heavenly Father! Go openly before Him and spend time with Him. He might even show us things about ourselves that we will need to *admit* and *quit*. After all, we can trust God. RIGHT?

READY? Here we go!

Personal Examination

This is a survey to help you examine yourself and assess your spiritual growth. This survey is between you and the Holy Spirit. (Be true to yourself.) This is an open-life exam.

"Examine yourselves, whether ye be in the faith; prove your own selves. Know ye not your own selves, how that Jesus Christ is in you, except ye be reprobates" (2 Corinthians 13:5).

1. Did you ever <u>admit</u> you are a sinner; <u>believe</u> in the Lord Jesus Christ and <u>believe</u> that He has cleansed you from your sins; and did you publicly <u>confess</u> Jesus as Lord and Savior of your life?
   _____

2. When is your spiritual birthday? (MM/DD/YY)
   _____

3. Who led you to your decision to accept Christ into your life? _____

4. Do you still have all your same old friends after accepting Christ?
   _____

5. Do you have any new friends after accepting Christ?
   _____

6. Do you attend the same church, or did you have to move to a Bible-believing church so that you could be spiritually fed?
   _____

7. Do you still go to the same social gatherings for the same purpose as you did before you accepted Christ?
   _____

8. Do you still enjoy the same bad habits that you had before accepting Christ?
   _____

9. If your answer to #8 is yes, go back to question #1.
   _____

10. Do you still read the same books, use the same vulgar language, and enjoy the same movies, etc., after accepting Christ? _____ If yes, go back to #1. (Think).

11. Do you spend more time now reading your Bible, praying, and meditating than when you first accepted Christ?
    _____

12. Is there anyone who you have not yet forgiven?
    _____

13. Does the Holy Spirit convict you of your sins? _____

14. Do you agree with the Holy Spirit that sin is sin? _____

15. Do you immediately repent from revealed sin? _____

16. Do you respect those who have the rule and authority over you? _____

17. Do you tithe (include more than just your money)? _____

18. Do you know what your spiritual gifts are?
    _____

19. Do you know your purpose or destiny in life?
    _____

20. Have you ever led anyone to Christ? If not, did you try? _____

21. Are you happy about your walk with the Lord, or are you bored?
    _____

22. Are you willing to die for the sake of Christ?_____

23. Do you have at least one earthly friend in which you can confide? _____

24. Did you learn anything about yourself as you responded to this survey? _____

25. Do you really, really love Jesus? _____

26. If you had one life to live and today was the last day of your life, what would you do differently? I hate to burst your bubble, BUT THIS IS A STRONG POSSIBILITY! So what would you REALLY do differently?

"In quietness and in confidence shall be your strength" (Isaiah 30:15).

Evelyn Murray Drayton

Facts About Myself

(The Reader)

1. I know that I am saved because _____

2. I accepted Jesus Christ into my heart on _____ (date)

3. The person who led me to Christ is _____

4. My favorite Scriptures are _____

5. My best prayer and meditation time is:
    o Morning (time) _____
    o Evening (time) _____
    o Late at night (time) _____
    o Other (time) _____

6. The person who inspires me the most is _____

7. My favorite spiritual song is _____

8. I have witnessed and won (#) ____ people to the Kingdom of Jesus Christ and realize that the best fishing spot for me to win SOULS is _____ (for example, the mall, school, concert, home, and so forth)

9. I read the Bible ____ often ____ occasionally ____ daily ____ seldom

10. The biggest scar that I must move beyond:

11. I incurred this scar when _____

12. I know that my spiritual gift to the Body of Christ is _____

Reading Journal

My purpose for reading this book:

Now that I have read this book, it seems to me:
Points of interest:

Were those points relevant and useful?

For Future Reference:
Page Number_____
Chapter _____
Paragraph _____

Page Number_____
Chapter _____
Paragraph _____

Page Number_____
Chapter _____
Paragraph _____

About the Author

Evangelist Evelyn Murray Drayton is your ordained minister of potential and possibilities. She is an acclaimed published author, inspirational speaker, Bible teacher, recording artist, wife, mother of two boys, and a woman of character and integrity. Having survived a 2013 near-death experience, she is now a compelling advocate for spiritual, emotional, mental, and physical encouragement to help you overcome adversities and challenges in life. She inspires, encourages, and empowers others to first seek Christ and reach their full potential and pursue possibilities.

Evelyn earned a master's degree in theology and a doctorate degree in Christian counseling from Cathedral Bible College in Myrtle Beach, South Carolina. She did further studies at Erskine Theological Seminary in Due West, South Carolina.

Evelyn is featured on various television programs and conducts live radio and blog talk Internet interviews. Her excellent leadership has helped to catapult other ministries to the forefront. Her prolific words are soothing, but powerful, and have captured the hearts of many. She counts it a privilege and an honor to share the Gospel using the Bible, her writing, and her music to help implement and accomplish ministry endeavors.

Evelyn has recorded several inspirational songs that have blessed listeners over the airwaves, and her two recent single recordings are titled, **Tell Somebody** and **Liquid Love**. She is the author of several published works, titled **I Had to Die Exposing Witchcraft in the Church, Silent Speaker, Feathered Wisdom, Sweet Success After Bitter Defeat, Watermelon Faith, Beyond Our Scars, And Suddenly,** and this most recent book, titled

Anything's Possible: The 47-Day Prophecy. Her work is listed on Amazon.com and other online portals.

Evelyn enjoys Bible teaching, reading, writing, and helping others. In addition to her biblical quotes, she loves the words of Oprah Winfrey: "Do the thing you cannot do. Fail at it. Try again. Do better the second time."

Reared in Clarendon County, Evelyn is happily married to Russell Drayton, and has been for over 25 years, and is proud to be a part of the Plantersville Community of Georgetown, South Carolina. She and Russell are proud of their two sons, Justin and Nicholas.

You may contact the author for books, music, or for various speaking engagements:

> Evangelist Evelyn Murray Drayton
> 876 Ford Village Road
> Georgetown, SC 29440
> Telephone: 843-546-4057
> E-mail: draytonevelyn@yahoo.com
> Website: www.evelyndrayton.org

OTHER PRODUCTS

Order from www.Amazon.com and other online portals.

And Suddenly…
ISBN: 978-0-615-75348-5

Watermelon Faith
ISBN: 978-1-60791-029-9

Sweet Success After Bitter Defeat
ISBN: 978-1-60266-763-1

Silent Speaker
ISBN: 1-4208-5457-7

Beyond Our Scars
ISBN: 9781609574765

Evelyn Murray Drayton

Feathered Wisdom
ISBN: 1-59453-811-5

I Had To Die Exposing
Witchcraft In The Church
ISBN: 1-4184-2021-2

Don't Burn Down   *Liquid Love*
My Bridge   *Music - single*
Music - CD

Special Notes

Special Notes

www.ingramcontent.com/pod-product-compliance
Lightning Source LLC
Chambersburg PA
CBHW071617080526
44588CB00010B/1157